D1554501

MAKE THE
BIG TIME
WHERE YOU ARE!

FROSTY WESTERING

Cover design by Terry Marks
Edited by Thomas Womack

MAKE THE BIG TIME WHERE YOU ARE
© by Frosty Westering
Published by Big Five Productions

Printed in the United States

First printing 1990

*To Donna my loving wife and
mother of our five young
adults, with all my love —
she always makes
the Big Time where we are.*

The Adventure

The Challenge .... i.

1. A Hammer and Chisel 1

2. #1 or No One 23

3. The Three-Sided Coin 41

4. Striving and Arriving 51

5. Is It Really a Good Day? 61

6. The Double-Edged Sword 75

7. A Touch of Class 83

8. A Ride in the Country 99

9. Contented Cows 107

10. It's Your Call 125

* * * * * * * * * * *

The Challenge

A great many people spend their entire lives looking for the so-called BIG TIME. They chase many illusions of grandeur and play countless games that appear to be THE BIG TIME — only to find themselves frustrated, disillusioned and unfulfilled. Other people believe they never had a chance to get there, so they live their lives feeling like they never made it and always wondering what it would have been like.

THE BIG TIME is actually a paradoxical puzzle, and like every puzzle it is made up of many pieces. Some of them I'm sure you have seen before; others may appear familiar, yet have a slightly different shape; while other pieces will be entirely new.

We are going to put this puzzle together, and when we complete it — all of a sudden the true picture of THE BIG TIME will appear. You will then understand and be able to apply it to your own life. When you do, exciting things begin to

happen. You will have more joy and fulfillment. You will perform what you do at a higher level. And as a by-product, you will have a new positive feeling about yourself and your place in life.

It is exciting for me to share the BIG TIME idea with you in this book — a book that I believe can change your life. Yes, that's what I said: change your life. That's a powerful statement, but this is a powerful idea.

My challenge to you is this: Keep an open mind — don't be afraid to change — and be willing to take a look at fulfillment, success, and THE BIG TIME for what they really can be.

Are you ready?

Let's turn the page and begin our adventure together.

FROSTY

Chapter 1

A Hammer and Chisel

THE blustery rainstorm came upon us quite suddenly during the morning as we were traveling up the two-lane mountain highway. The dry pavement of a few miles back had now become wet and slick, but the steady beat of the windshield wipers kept our vision clear as we drove into a short winding canyon. Approaching a sharp zigzag curve, we heard a loud rumbling sound above us. Within seconds, it happened — a huge rock came thundering down the canyon wall just ahead of us. It hit on the side of the road with a resounding crash and careened onto the highway. Pieces of it flew in all directions. Gary slammed on the brakes, we skidded — and skidded, and skidded — and finally came to an abrupt stop less than two feet from the giant fallen rock. I bowed my head in silent prayer. Time seemed to stand still. When I looked up I saw Gary staring at me. Neither of us spoke a word for a few moments. I finally said, "I now know what those road signs really mean."

"What signs?"

"You know — the ones that say, 'Watch for Falling Rocks.'"

We both smiled, and yet realized how within a matter of seconds we could have been victims of a falling rock. It was at least eight feet high and blocked two-thirds of the highway.

There were no other cars visible, so Gary backed up and drove around it. The rain had now let up. I got out and stayed near the rock to alert any other cars, while Gary drove back a few miles to a small gas station we had passed to call the highway patrol. He was back shortly and we directed the oncoming cars around the big rock until the patrolmen arrived in about half an hour. As we were ready to continue our trip, I looked again at the huge rock, and picked up two small pieces that had chipped off.

It was midmorning when we pulled up to the picturesque mountain cabin. We had driven less than an hour from the fallen rock and were now in a beautiful mountain setting some five miles off the main highway. The weather was cool and the sky was now clear.

As we got out of the car we decided to hike up through the big trees to a small lake nestled against the snow-capped mountain peaks. It was a picture-book setting and a great way to start our adventure.

Gary was a sharp, successful businessman and a friend of mine whom I had met several years ago. We had similar interests, and our friendship and fellowship had grown over the past few years. I had previously shared THE BIG TIME idea with him, and while he didn't understand much about it, he was very intrigued and interested. He had invited me to go on this trip to the mountains to further discuss and learn more it.

Returning to the car, we took out our personal gear and went into the cozy two-bedroom cabin. After getting our belongings unpacked and having a bite to eat, we built a fire in the large, rugged fireplace that was the focal point of one end of the cabin. We sat down in two big overstuffed chairs near the fire. The wood was now crackling as the flames burned brightly.

"You know, Gary, sitting by a fire like this creates a sense of relaxation and reflection. It just makes you feel good — and I really appreciate being able to come with you on this breakaway experience."

"Frosty, that's what that big rock did this morning — break away — and believe me, that was an experience."

"That's for sure, and we were very fortunate. You know, most people would call this a retreat rather than a breakaway. But to me, a retreat is a passive and negative way to relate an experience.

A breakaway creates a positive feeling of anticipation and adventure — and that's what I believe we are going to have together."

"The pleasure of being on this breakaway is all mine. I've been interested in talking to you about this BIG TIME idea of yours for a long time. I've even mentioned it to my wife and family as well as my business associates, and they are all anxious for me to share it with them when I return."

"This BIG TIME idea is unique and powerful, and I definitely believe it can change any person's life for the better when they really understand it, believe it, and — 'just do it.'"

"Frosty, I want you to know that while I am intrigued by this idea, I'm not sure you really can MAKE THE BIG TIME WHERE YOU ARE. I am relatively successful in the business world, and I know I'm not in THE BIG TIME. I'm also sure that the vast majority of other people aren't either. I am interested, but it'll take a lot of convincing for me to change my way of thinking. I'm sure you've heard the saying: 'You can lead a horse to water, but you can't make him drink.'"

"But, Gary — you can sure make him thirsty."

He raised his eyebrows and smiled.

"I'm sure you've heard or read about many of these concepts we are going to talk about.

However, just knowing about them has no real pay value. The key is in understanding and believing in them, for this is what motivates us to put them all together and use them. It's like a puzzle: You can have all the pieces, but until you actually put them together you really don't have anything. Each one of these concepts is like a piece of a puzzle, and when we put them all together the true picture of THE BIG TIME will suddenly appear."

"That's an interesting way to put it."

"It's going to be both an interesting and exciting adventure. You may not at first understand all of the pieces we put in the BIG TIME puzzle. But, it's the big picture that really counts, and it takes time to really see it. When you do — you'll know exactly what I mean."

Gary nodded his head and settled back more into his chair as the fire continued to burn brightly.

"I've always liked to share stories to make a key point, because a story allows you to visualize a situation in your mind's eye and follow it through to the end." A smile slowly crept across Gary's face; he had heard a few of "Frosty's stories" before.

"Let me tell you a classic one that relates in a very unique way to the huge rock that fell in front of us earlier this morning." I pulled out the two rock chips I had picked up on the highway and handed one to Gary. "This story illustrates the exciting challenge we have ahead of us," and I began the story:

Michael was a young man from a small town who was extremely talented with a hammer and chisel. He could take a rock and create any figure you could imagine. His creations were a marvel for all who saw them, and his business was very successful.

In spite of his success, Michael always had the feeling that the talent with his hammer and chisel was really insignificant. He wanted to be someone else...somewhere else. He desired to be in THE BIG TIME.

One afternoon while working on one of his creations, he became quite weary. He laid down his hammer and chisel and took a nap. While sleeping, a genie appeared to him in a dream and promised to grant him three wishes to fulfill his desire to be in THE BIG TIME. Michael was ecstatic. He looked up and immediately saw the sun in the sky...big, powerful and dominating the earth. This was it; he wanted to be the sun. So Michael became the sun —

THE BIG TIME.

After several days, however, many cloud formations appeared and blocked his power and view of the earth. It was obvious to him now that the sun was not really THE BIG TIME. Through the gaps in the clouds he could see a large rambling river. He saw the power and immense size of the river flowing through the large canyons and broad valleys. He wanted to be the river, the river was THE BIG TIME so Michael became the river.

One day while flowing through a long canyon, he noticed a large group of people admiring a huge rock of many colors that rose high above him. He saw the majesty and stability of this impressive rock. This is it, he thought. The rock is THE BIG TIME. So he used his third and final wish to become the rock.

He had finally arrived — he was in THE BIG TIME. He looked out at the world and glowed with pride as people continued to admire him; finally he was happy.

It wasn't long after becoming the rock however, that something startling happened. As the sun rose to start a new day, Michael felt a chip, chip, chipping and heard a tap, tap, tapping sound coming from one of his colorful sides. He looked down and couldn't believe what he saw — **a young man carving away with his hammer and chisel.**

I paused for a few moments and looked into Gary's eyes. "What we are really talking about is this: *What you see is not always what you get.*"

"This hammer and chisel story is where we begin to take our first look at the fascinating paradox of THE BIG TIME. Believe me, we will see the many illusions and elusive qualities of this so called place." He looked at the small rock chip in his hand for several moments, nodded his head, smiled, and then opened a large, brown notebook and started to take some notes.

"The dictionary defines *paradox* as a statement that is self-contradictory and is contrary to popular belief. That's what Michael, our young man in the story, found out; when he got there, it wasn't what he thought it would be. This helps us start understanding the secret of THE BIG TIME paradox. The secret is —

THE BIG TIME IS NOT A PLACE;

IT'S A STATE OF THE HEART.

I'm not talking about our physical heart that pumps our blood some seventy-plus times a minute. I'm talking about the heart that is the center and source of our innermost thoughts and feelings — the heart that radiates our entire being. Many people never really know their heart, that dynamic spirit that generates hope, faith, and love. You see, <u>THE BIG TIME is not something you get — it's something you become</u>. Those people who believe it's a place find out that once they get *THERE*, then it disappears. They find *it* was only an illusion, the illusion that THE BIG TIME is a destination rather than a journey. The adventurous road always continues on, and wherever we are on our journey through life, we can make it THE BIG TIME."

Gary thought for a moment and then wrote again in his notes.

"The first thing we have to do in putting THE BIG TIME puzzle together is to use a power we all possess. Most people do not recognize this as a power and have struggled through many different situations in their lives; yet when they do become aware of it and use it in a positive way, they begin to see many exciting changes taking place. What we are talking about is —

THE POWER OF CHOICE."

"I've never thought of choice as being a power."

"It is, believe me, it is. It's one of God's greatest gifts. That's really what we're talking about, choosing THE BIG TIME. It's our ability to choose our actions and reactions in our daily lives that frees us up to experience the natural highs that God intended us to have. It has a powerful influence on our feelings, actions and lifestyle. Most people are not able to make these choices because they believe the BIG TIME is a place, and it seems everybody is telling them where it is and how to get there. This thought process becomes a mindset that limits their perspective of life. However, our true thoughts and beliefs come from our heart, not from our head. The expression 'change of heart' means our inner being changes and we then choose to change our minds. When we begin to realize this, we can start to choose our thoughts, rather than just conforming for the sake of going along with others."

"I know I've done that many times," Gary confided.

"We all have, but when we begin to see the excitement we can generate by listening to our heart — we grow in new ways. This allows us to experience many natural highs in our daily lives that we didn't know existed. We then start to understand what THE BIG TIME feeling really is."

Several years ago, while on vacation, my wife, Donna, and I woke up early sixish on a warm summer morning and took a walk on a nearby beach. We walked for some forty-five minutes enjoying the sights, sounds and feelings of the day. As we looked ahead, we saw a small unique cafe right on the water's edge. When we came to it, we decided to go in and have breakfast. We sat down at one of the few empty tables. The young waitress came over and took our order, and within a few minutes she brought our food. I had ordered my favorite: extra-crisp bacon, eggs sunnyside up, and toastie toast. When she sat our orders down, I noticed right away everything was perfect — the eggs were just right, the bacon cooked just like I liked it and the toast was toastie. So many times, as you know, food does not come exactly as ordered; but this was made precisely to order. I took two dollars from my billfold and caught the attention of our waitress. She came over to our table and I told her that this breakfast was exceptional and I wanted to tip the cook. She said, "Excuse me, no one tips the cook; you tip the waitress." I said, "We'll tip you all right; but this cook is outstanding. Can I take it back to him?" She replied, "You can't go into the kitchen." I answered, "Then how are we going to do this?"

She looked at me rather foolishly, took the tip, and went to the kitchen. In a few seconds the cook came out through the swinging kitchen doors. He was a big man with a white outfit and a typical chef's hat. The waitress pointed to our table, and he immediately came over to us and said, "I'd like to meet you, my name is John." I replied, "I'm Frosty and this is my wife, Donna." He nodded and looked in my eyes and said, "Frosty, I want you to know you've made my day. No, you've made my week; actually you've made my job. I take real pride in preparing every order just as it's desired, every little request. I get paid a good wage but I've never had anyone, let alone a customer (who I really cook for), tell me I was doing a good job. This tip from you is really special. I'm going to frame these two dollar bills and put them over my grill with the caption, 'A tip from Frosty' — it means that much to me." I replied, "John, you're really a pro, you take pride in your profession. Whether others recognize it or not, continue to give it your best shot and enjoy the trip — MAKE THE BIG TIME WHERE YOU ARE." John's eyes lit up. "I like that — I won't forget this day." He smiled. I stood up and we exchanged a big hug and a warm friendly handshake.

"Frosty, I just never realized how important it is to really feel good about what you are doing; to actually take pride in your profession by doing your best. When someone recognizes it and lets you know it, like you did with John — what a difference it makes."

"You're right on target. Sincere recognition is one of our basic needs and most of us never receive enough of it. The put-up game that I played with John creates a natural high in helping people feel good about themselves. You see, Gary, I have played and coached games all my life; and I've found that when you integrate the game concept into life situations, you have so much more enjoyment in what you do. This put-up game can be played in various ways. You can affirm, appreciate, compliment, encourage or praise. These are the BIG 5 fundamentals of the put-up game. I'm not talking about the phony folks who put up people for selfish reasons or flatter people for ulterior motives — I'm talking about the right stuff, genuine unselfish caring."

"This all sounds good, but who really wants to do that? This can take time and distract you from your own priorities. Who can go around looking for what others are doing? Besides, it isn't easy to do, and nobody does it much anyway. It's a jungle out there — you've got to look out for <u>yourself</u>. It's survival of the fittest."

"Gary — it's more than surviving; it's enjoying and experiencing success in new ways. Here we have ourselves another paradox: Our ability to put-up someone else is directly related to the way we see our own self."

"What do you mean by that?"

"I mean that when we start looking for and acknowledging the right stuff in others, it frees us up to rise above our own self-centeredness. As we make others feel good about themselves, the desire to produce good results increases. And a by-product is that we feel better about ourselves and our own performance increases. We are now focusing on the right stuff, and it works both ways: The more you give, the more you receive."

"The put-up game, just like a football game, takes practice — the right kind of practice. Put-ups, just like anything else, have to be learned; they have to become a habit — and believe me, they don't just happen. There are many ways to play this game, other than verbal. Many physical gestures such as a thumbs-up, a give-me-five, a hug, or a nod of the head with a smile — all communicate effectively. Written put-ups work too — from short notes to telegrams. You get the idea. The name of the game is DO IT NOW!

Gary shook his head. "This is sure a different way to look at relationships."

"It sure is. And by the way, do you know that many people don't really know how to accept a put-up? Without realizing it, they will put-down the person who is putting them up. They either say nothing at all or say all kinds of things but the right thing — which is a simple, sincere thank you. You can say more, but really those two words are the key. This shows that you accept it and recognize the person who gave the put-up."

He sat back, reflected on what we had discussed, and then wrote in his notebook.

"There are other games out there that actually take away natural highs and the BIG TIME feeling. One of these is the put-down game. Put-downs are all around us and we can become involved in them just by association. This game actually reflects a person's own self-centeredness and inadequacies without his even being aware of it. It can easily become a self-fulfilling prophecy: By putting others down, we end up putting ourselves down. All of us play a version of this game at different times. I remember so well a time I played a classic put-down game when I was coaching my oldest son Brad."

He was an outstanding quarterback and the father-son combination drew quite a bit of media attention. This particular experience happened during Brad's first year of playing varsity college football. Our senior quarterback separated his shoulder and was out for the season. Brad moved from the back-up role to that of starting quarterback. This was it, the father-son, coach-quarterback combination. I've always believed that the put-up game is one of the keys to building confidence and in motivating an individual to reach their potential, and now I was being tested to see if I could walk my talk with my own son. It's very easy to lose your perspective with your own family when you and everyone else have high expectations. Many times you end up playing the no-win perfection game and struggling all the way. That's just what I did. It was like walking on a tight rope — and here's how I fell off . . . .

Brad got off to a great start. He led us to four straight victories and a national ranking in our division. It was mid-season and our big homecoming game. All the old grads and everyone connected with the University were involved in the pre-game hoopla and homecoming activities. The game was against the strong state university team and everyone knew it would be a good one.

We kicked off and our defense forced them to punt on the first series of downs. We took over the ball on our own thirty-five yard line. On second down, Brad threw his first pass of the game — it was intercepted and returned to the forty-five yard line. As he came out of the game I went over to Brad and patted him on the back and told him, 'It's O.K. We'll do it next time — keep your head up.' We then got the ball right back three plays later on a recovered fumble and Brad went back into the game. On third down, he threw his second pass of the game — it was intercepted. When he came to the sidelines, I again went over to him and did the same as before, telling him it was O.K. But — that really wasn't how I felt. We had worked on these plays all week and I felt that he wasn't reading the defenses and was forcing his passes to covered receivers. I was losing my coaching cool.

Our defense, however, was playing great and forced another punt. Once again we got the ball at mid-field. On first down, we decided to throw the long bomb. Brad faded back and threw his third pass of the game — *INTERCEPTED*. As our offense was coming off the field, I lost my poise and started out on the field to meet Brad. The referee, the fans in the stands, and you name it, they all saw me going out on the field. The ref threw the penalty flag but before he got to me, I got to Brad. I looked him in the eye and yelled, "Brad, what's the matter with you? That's your third interception." He answered with a quick, firm voice, "I can count, Dad." The referee was now right behind me as I said to Brad, "You're passing the ball to the wrong guys" (now that's real coaching), but before I could say another word, Brad responded with one of the best one-line comebacks I have ever heard. He looked me in the eye and said, "Dad, those are the only guys that are open."

Gary laughed.

The ref about lost it too, trying not to laugh out loud. As we jogged off the field, I looked up in the stands and realized that up there was where I really should have been. When Brad needed me most to help him work through a tough, frustrating situation, I was no help at all. The fact was that I was putting him down, when that was the last thing he needed to build up his confidence. I was struggling in a different way and was definitely out of character. It wasn't so much *what* I said, but *how* I said it. I should have been up in the stands selling popcorn and peanuts.

"The interesting postscript to this whole experience, was when we looked at the game films the next day. We saw that the guys on the other team *were* the only ones open!!"

Gary smiled and asked, "How did the game come out?"

"We actually won it on the scoreboard, but I really struggled with my role the entire game, for I had lost the joy of the competitive experience because of unrealistic expectations I had for my son. High-level expectations are tricky, and we need to understand them — for when we start to play the no-win perfection game, it causes us to lose that joy and performance level we value so much."

He looked at me intently.

"Many people have been playing this put-down game so long it's actually become part of them. They may try to play the put-up game, but they always seem to revert back. We are all creatures of habit, and our habits of thought directly affect our physical ones. Habits start like twigs that are easily broken; but through continued use they turn into steel rods which are extremely difficult to break. Criticism and negative put-downs become steel habits which can turn into cynicism. And this, I'm sorry to say, has become the dominant trait of many people today. They believe you have to blow out other's candles so their own will shine brighter. These people don't realize that in this kind of game one blow and they could all be out — it's a no-win game. The truth is, when you light other's candles, we all shine brighter — and that's what the put-up game is all about. This simple yet meaningful experience of lighting the cook's candle is what we are talking about. John started to realize that the pride in his performance as a cook was making his position BIG TIME; and since no one really had acknowledged his special efforts, it took a situation like this to give him that BIG TIME feeling. I hope you are beginning to see how the games you play are directly related to the idea of MAKING THE BIG TIME WHERE YOU ARE. It starts with those innermost feelings in your heart that actually transform your mind. This in turn affects your actions, and it makes all the difference in the world in the way you live each day of your life, regardless of your position."

"I'm starting to get the feel of your BIG TIME idea. This way of looking at it is certainly different, and you have definitely stimulated my thinking."

He thought to himself and then underlined in his notes,

"The Big Time is not a place;

it's the state of your heart."

"It's not something you get;

it's something you become."

Chapter 2

#1 or No One

WE put more logs on the fire, and the golden flames danced brightly again as we settled back into our chairs.

"Gary, there are many people in our society today who are caught up in what's called the '#1 or No One' mindset. They believe that if they're not the best, the champion, the first-place finisher, they are really a *no one* — second place or any other place has no place in their book. This belief is based on the premise that there is no real success in life unless they are #1. A mindset of this type sees only the outcome as important — the process has to be endured. They constantly compare themselves to others and always have to prove themselves superior to feel secure and successful. Tension and pressure are often present, and if they or whomever they support are not #1, they become defensive and resentful. Without their being aware of it, the fear of failure is their primary motivator, and most of the time it has a negative effect on their thoughts, feelings, and actions.

"An ironical aspect of this kind of thinking is that when they do gain comparison success and get in the so-called 'top echelon,' they many times become arrogant, self-centered, and even cocky. A good example of this is Gary Larson's *Far Side* cartoon of General Custer's last group photo. Did you ever see it?"

He shook his head.

I took it out of a folder.

THE FAR SIDE   By GARY LARSON

June 24, 1876: Custer's last group photo

Gary chuckled.

"It's a classic — all that we're #1 stuff. Then, as we remember, they all went out and got massacred. Custer's group didn't know that they really didn't know. And believe me there are many times in our lives that we are the same way — we really don't know we have other choices to make. Let's pick up another piece of THE BIG TIME puzzle and see how it fits into the picture. Let's look at an eagle."

"An eagle?"

Donald was a young farmer who lived on a farm that spread out over the broad flatlands beneath a high cliff. One morning as he drove down the road next to the cliff, he noticed a nest-like object of sticks and grassy-type material lying by the side of the road. He stopped and went over, and as he picked it up he saw a baby eagle tucked into the broken nest. He looked up the high cliff, but couldn't see where the nest had fallen from. He sat the nest and the eaglet on a low cliff ledge. The next day he found the nest by the road again with the baby eagle in it. He picked up the baby eagle and decided to take it back to his farm yard. When he arrived, he looked around for a place to put it. His eyes stopped at the chicken pen where all the baby chicks were. There was no roof on the pen — the eaglet could fly away when it was ready. Thus he decided this was the place and put the baby eagle in with the young chicks. Time went by. The little eagle had now grown much larger than the young chickens in the pen.

One day Roger, a neighbor, came over to visit and noticed the young eagle in the chicken pen. He asked Don about the eagle and they both agreed it really did not belong with the chickens and should start to fly as young eagles do. Even though there was no roof on the pen, the young eagle had remained there. Roger picked up the eagle and took him outside the pen, held him high over his head, and gave him a toss into the air. The eagle dropped to the ground like a rock and shuffled back into the chicken pen. They tried this maneuver several more times, with the same results. Always the young eagle returned to the chicken pen.

Several weeks later Roger came back to visit Donald again. This time he had what he considered a better idea on how to help the young eagle fly. He convinced Donald that all they had to do was to get the young eagle to spread its wings and it would then fly. The way to do this was to take the eagle to the top of the cliff and toss it off. Its wings would then spread out, and it would be able to fly. Donald agreed, so both men climbed the side of the cliff behind the farmyard, taking the young eagle with them. They finally came to the top of the cliff with the entire farm in view. Roger tossed the young eagle over the edge of the cliff. It fell like a rock toward the farmyard below. Both farmers looked in despair, anticipating that they had made a big mistake and that the young eagle was going to be crushed and die.

However, half way down in its fall from the high cliff, the young eagle's wings opened and it went into a perfect glide. The two farmers looked at each other with a big smile on their faces as the eagle circled through the air over the farmyard. However, as the eagle neared the ground, they noticed it was gliding directly toward the chicken pen. The young eagle came closer and closer to the pen preparing to settle on the ground with the chicks. But at the last instant, it flapped its wings and started back up toward the sky. Again and again the young eagle flapped its wings until it soared high above the cliff and out of sight.

"Did you get the message, Gary?"

"I believe so — regardless of its choice, the eagle would never be the same again."

"That's exactly it. The eagle learned it could fly, and then chose to fly away like a true eagle. If it had chosen to go back to the chicken pen, it would not have been *the same eagle;* for then it would have been an eagle in the chicken pen and not a chicken as it thought it was before. That's what I believe is going to happen to you. When you get the BIG TIME puzzle together, you will find you are going to have another choice, a choice that right now you really don't know you have — then, like the eagle, regardless of which choice you make, you'll never be the same. We are going to take a look at two success roads. One is a version of a road you now know; the other is a new and different one where you will see fulfillment and THE BIG TIME in a new perspective."

"Frosty, I'm not sure what you mean."

"What I mean is this: The majority of people, young and old, struggle in far too many areas of their daily lives. They actually miss out on countless numbers of natural highs in ordinary things that are all around them. They think like the eagle when it was in the chicken pen, which really limits their potential for fulfillment. What we're talking about is winning. Many people don't know what it's like to feel like a winner because they really don't know what a winner is. I don't mean a winner in a sports contest or some business deal, but a winner where it really counts — in the game of life. In fact, there are many athletes, business people, and you name it who win in their own specific arena but do not know how to live a winning lifestyle in their own personal lives. As a result, they get all bent out of shape and they struggle with many things in their lives which they don't need to. Once we learn what winning in everyday life is all about, we can then make new choices that can change our lives in new and exciting ways."

"I know there have been numerous times when I've been caught in that trap and haven't felt very good about myself."

"We all have. But now, let's take a good look at some choices that can make a difference in what we focus on and think about. We will then realize how much effect it can have on us and how we feel about ourselves. Let's talk about two different models of winning — and just like the young eagle, we'll find we have an important choice to make. Let's go back to the '#1 or no one' mindset. This concept is based on one particular model of winning. It has been perpetuated through the years and has been accepted by many as the only model of winning. This concept is based solely on comparison success. The goal is to win in whatever we do by defeating others. In other words, how am I doing compared to the next guy, or anyone and everyone? If I beat someone or anyone, I'm a winner. If I lose to someone or anyone, I'm a loser. I'm O.K. if I win, but not O.K. if I lose. The bottom line of this model is that the winner is everything, the loser is nothing; #1 or no one — you're either in the penthouse or the outhouse."

Gary smiled.

"I believe the goal of this model of winning is self-defeating the greatest percentage of the time, and in reality has produced few real winners in life. In sports there is only one team that ever wins their last game and are the champions — in this mindset all the rest are considered losers. It's ironic that in this model, those who do win it all find that the feeling is soon gone as they get caught in the web of time and place and are soon forgotten or overshadowed. Fame is very fragile and fleeting. Most people don't even remember who won the World Series or the Super Bowl a few years ago. The idea of this road to success makes winning actually a mirage, a vivid illusion, like Michael with his dream of THE BIG TIME — it really wasn't what he thought it was."

"Frosty, I hear what you're saying, but that's the way it is and that's the way people think. It's the old 'king of the hill.'"

"It's still a no-win game; the 'king of the hill' falls off just like Humpty Dumpty did, and then, believe me, there's usually nothing left. If all we do is endure or tolerate the trip to a so-called destination, we've really missed the boat. A better way to put it is: We're on the boat, but we are seasick most of the time. Let's look at another model of winning that has a different focus and goal. When we understand, believe, and apply this model to our lives, a subtle yet dramatic change starts to take place in us that frees us up to enjoy life more. And to our surprise, we perform at higher levels. The goal of this model is ACHIEVEMENT — achievement within our own self, not to win over others as in the other model. It focuses on where the actual control of our performance is. Statistics from various fields of endeavor show that the greatest percentage of time we actually defeat ourselves. We do not hit the targets that are right in front of us or perform near our capacity because we are focusing our energies and talents in the wrong place. Let's see if this poem puts it into perspective:"

The Enemy We Face

The enemy I had, I didn't even know.
He followed me unseen, wherever I would go.

He blocked my plans, he blocked my way,
He countered me, even before I could say.

Each time I would make the effort to try,
He made me afraid, so I'd let things pass by.

One night I caught him and grabbed for his mask;
I wanted to see, I wanted to ask.

But to my amazement as I looked at his face,
It was me that I saw, and I prayed for GOD'S GRACE.

The enemy who had been hiding inside,
I finally let go of, and the enemy died.

My new friend inside shares an exciting new way:
He says "YES WE CAN" as we start out each day.

Our SPIRIT in life is the KEY TO IT ALL.
Our BELIEF deep inside picks us up when we fall.

I can run LIFE'S RACE with a CALM INNER PEACE.
I GO FOR IT NOW WITH TOTAL RELEASE.

"This poem shows us where our point of effort should be in all that we do in relation to where the control is — within ourselves. The name of the game is actually 'ME vs. ME' and not 'ME against THE WORLD.' When I zero in on this idea, my confidence and performance start going up.

"All of us have a gap between what we can be and what we are. This gap has been commonly called the Potential/Performance Gap." I took out a marker and made the basic diagram of the GAP.

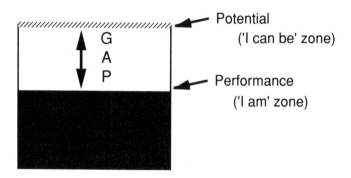

"The top dotted line indicates our potential (the 'I can be' zone), and a bottom solid line indicates our performance (the 'I am zone.') The space between these two lines is the GAP between what I can be and what I am. The key to closing this GAP is found in the acronym itself."

G is for **Goal-sets** that motivate and challenge us.

A is for **Attitude** which is our self-fulfilling prophesy — for whether we think we can or think we can't, we're usually right.

P is for **Perserverance** which develops mental toughness and builds our character.

"We can reach higher performance levels and close our **GAP** as we continually apply these three qualities to our lives."

I picked up a plaque that I had laid against my chair and handed it to Gary. He read it aloud:

> ## The Real Measure of Me Is Not *What I Can Do in Comparison to Others* But *What I Can Do in Comparison to My Own Best Self*

"That's it — that's what we're talking about — the challenge of our best self. Let's look at a diagram of these two models of winning together and see if we really understand what we're talking about." I took the chart from my briefcase and showed it to him.

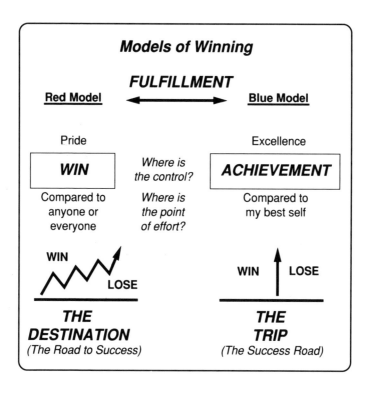

"In the Red Model #1 or No One — the goal is coming out on top by defeating anyone and everyone. People using this model always measure their own worth compared to others. Their performance level will correspond to the level of their competition, and actually goes up and down like a yo-yo as shown on the model. The high-level competitive experience goes right by them, due to the fact that all they are doing is playing to win. If they do experience repeated successes, it

can easily put them on an ego trip. The by-product
of this is inconsistent performances, and when a
losing cycle begins, as it will, the fear of failure
comes to the surface in the form of negative
feedback, tension and pressure. Everyone seems
to think the answer is to work harder. However,
that isn't it — the answer is a change in attitude
and model of winning."

"Does that mean striving to win is wrong?"
"I'll let you answer that question after we've
finished looking at the Blue Model that sees
winning in a different perspective. The goal of this
model is personal achievement — excellence and
winning become the by-products. The focus now
is on one's own personal or group performance,
not on others'. You seek to do your best compared
to your own best self, for this is where the real
control lies. As you achieve more in specific areas,
you then compete at higher levels. The by-product
is that by not defeating yourself and by competing
at a consistent level, you will reach excellence and
win in the competitive arena a much higher percent
of the time. In this model, you truly learn how to
enjoy the competitive experience. And believe it
or not — that's what brings out the best in you,
your family, your team, or your business."

"I'm not sure I understand."

"O.K., let's take another shot at it. Most people
use the Red Model of winning (comparison

success) because that is all they know. When they understand, believe, and experience the exciting pay value of the Blue Model (achievement success) they then change their focus and start challenging their best self in a new way. They now begin to really enjoy the competitive experience, resulting in exciting by-products — like not being afraid to fail and having more fulfillment in their lives — performing at higher levels and experiencing new levels of excellence — and desiring to care and share in new ways. The differences in the red and blue models of winning are where you put your focus and your point of effort. Here's an experience that really changed a man's life when he changed his model of winning."

A group of middle-aged businessmen asked me years ago if I would help them develop a personal fitness program. They all had physical examinations and we had our first meeting together in sweats, shoes, the whole works. I shared with them the key concept of competing against yourself: ME vs. ME — learning to challenge your best self and not others. After going over all the other areas of warm-up, stretching, and progressive workouts, I asked them to find out where their fitness levels were right now. I asked them to write down on a 3 X 5 card how far they believed they could jog at a constant pace before they would feel stress and then stop. I put flags around the track at each 110 yards, to help them estimate their distance. As we did this, Ralph, a short heavyset man, got up and started to leave. While the others were getting ready for their warm-up, I caught up to him and asked what was wrong. "Frosty," he said, "I'm embarrassed — all these other men are going out there and will jog so much further than I can. I'm a joke — I'm just not going to do it." "Ralph," I said, "I have shared with you how important it is to compete against yourself, to challenge yourself and not compare yourself to others. When you learn to do that, you will start to enjoy the challenge and competition of becoming your best self." "Frosty, that sounds good, but that isn't how it works — everyone compares you to others and in my case it's a no win." I looked Ralph in the eyes and said, "How far do you think you can jog before you feel stress?" He didn't answer. "Can you go one lap?" He shook his head. "How about a half lap?" "I couldn't do that," he said. "How about a straight-away?" Before he could respond, I looked and saw a big tree about fifty yards away. I said, "Ralph, how about the big tree?" He looked at the tree and replied, "I can make the tree." "Let's go," I shouted. So he and I jogged to the tree. As soon as we got there, I exclaimed, "Ralph, we made it — you're a *one-tree man.*" He gave me a puzzled look, but his eyes lit up when I said, "This is where you start, one tree." His look now turned into a smile and he said, "Frosty, you're right, this is where I start — I'm a one tree man."

Six weeks later Ralph was a 42-tree man.

He jogged near a wooded area and counted trees instead of laps. Forty-two trees was a little over one mile. His progress was exciting, and he loved the new challenge of ME vs. ME. He even placed a tiny tree in his office every time he reached a new one in his workout. Believe me, after a while *he had a jungle in there, and he loved it.*

Gary laughed heartily.

"You see, what Ralph had learned about winning has changed his life. Not just in jogging, but in everything. You can't convince him he's a No One just because he's not #1. He has learned the true fulfillment of the competitive experience: bringing out the best in ourselves and others. That's what MAKING THE BIG TIME WHERE YOU ARE is all about."

"You have a choice:
Are you going to fly,
or
are you going back
to the chicken pen?"

Chapter 3

The Three-Sided Coin

W E went into the kitchen for a snack and returned to our big chairs. The wood continued to crackle sporadically and burned brightly. As we sat down, I remarked, "We've put together the first pieces in our BIG TIME puzzle."

"I still don't see much of the big picture, Frosty, but you know, I already see that if I can just apply a few of these BIG TIME concepts to my golf game, I know I'll play better. I always get upset when I hook or slice on my drive, or overshoot a green, or three putt. I tend to get intimidated too easily by the course or who I'm playing with, and it affects my whole game."

"Believe me, Gary, many golfers are like that. When you get this BIG TIME puzzle put together, it will help not only your golf game but also any other game, including the big one — the game of life.

Now let's look at another important choice. How do football games begin?"

"With the kickoff."

"No, I mean before the kickoff."

"You mean the coin flip?"

"That's right, the coin flip. In fact, let's have a coin flip right now." I pulled out a quarter and got ready for the flip. "You call it."

"I'll take heads."

I flipped the coin and caught it in one hand, and instead of turning it over flat on the back of my opposite hand, as is often done, I turned it over, holding it between my fingers so that neither the heads or the tails was up but the edge of the coin. "Gary, the edge wins."

"Wait a minute; that's not the way to do it."

"You mean the edge can't win?"

"Come on, Frosty."

"In a coin flip, you're right. But we're not going to talk about a simple game of chance like a coin flip. We're going to talk about the third side of the coin, one that most people don't know or realize is even a side. We're talking about THE EDGE. That small edge that circles the entire coin really can make a great difference, not in a coin flip, but in our lives."

"I've heard lots of athletes talk about THE EDGE."

"Competitors in any field talk about THE EDGE. Some have called it the winning edge, others have called it the competitive edge. Regardless of what you call it, THE EDGE is what makes the difference in your performance in any walk of life. This is *what the best is all about.* Let's look at it from three different points of view, like the three sides of the coin that relate directly to the word 'best.' First off let's talk about the side of the coin that most people choose when we talk about best — that is, *being the best.* We discussed the '#1 or no one' idea before, but let's look again from the view of the three-sided coin. People who choose this side of the coin talk about, think about and go about — with all their time, talents, and efforts — trying to be #1 in whatever they do. To measure this they continually play the comparison game and are always searching for that road to success. The fallacy of this way of thinking is, as I said before, that we can't really control being #1. This side of the coin does not give you the edge. In fact, you really lose the edge. Being the best in anything is actually a by-product of the competitive experience and most people don't understand this. It is the result of a combination of various factors and one of the most important ones is not defeating ourselves.

The second side of the coin and the second view of best is *doing our best.* We need to realize that doing our best is more important than being the best, because we are now focusing on our real competition: ourselves. As I shared in the poem, we can put our energy and efforts where they belong — on ourselves, where they can have the greatest effect on our performance. In the many diverse competitive areas of our lives, most of the time *we beat ourselves*. We are out of focus and concentrating on the wrong target — our opponents. We cannot control them, but we can control ourselves, and when we really come to understand and believe this *we will adjust the way we compete.* That's really important. We now focus on key targets that we can hit. When we do this, our concentration and confidence are dramatically increased, thereby raising our level of performance. I realize there are times we are defeated on a scoreboard or in a business situation by an outstanding performance by our opponent. However, a high percent of the time, we actually beat ourselves through our own *errors in judgment, basic mistakes* and *improper use of our efforts.* There is a 20/80 rule that says 20% of what we do produces 80% of the results. Too many people don't know what the 20% really is that controls 80% of their performance. They focus on things that are out of their control or spend too much time on things that are insignificant. Each one of us needs to look at what we are doing and determine the key fundamentals that really do make a difference. We should then spend the majority of our time there. When we zero in on the key performance fundamentals of a particular situation, we are now working on that 20% that really controls the level of that 80% of our performance. It's like changing our aim from long-range, out-of-focus targets to short-range, clearly defined ones. We now zero in on the bull's eye and aim and fire away. When we do this, our performance improves remarkably — that is, *if we aim before we fire."*

"I know some of those fire - aim people in my business."

"Gary, they are in every business. They shoot from the hip and most of the time never come close to the bull's eye. The key to reaching excellence on a consistent basis is to keep shooting at those bull's eyes of our own specific targets, and *to be sure we aim before we fire*. When we do this, we put ourselves in position where being the best can become a bonafide by-product.

"The key question is, *'What is our best?'* and *'How do we bring out our best?'"* The first thing we need to realize is that *we can usually do much better than we think we can."*

He looked at me with raised eyebrows.

"'Potential' is difficult to measure. There are various tests: intelligence, fitness, skill, and other potential tests relating to specific performance.

However, there is another intangible quality in all of us that has far surpassed the results of these tests. That quality is an inner drive, a powerful drive, just waiting to be tapped. When it is, we become truly motivated and shift into another gear we didn't realize we had. Success in anything in life is largely mental — not mental intelligence but mental attitude and mental toughness. Both of these are essential ingredients for doing our best. Our attitude is our habit of thought, and is one of the keys to unlocking our potential. People live and die every day because of their attitudes and don't even know it. A winning attitude has to be learned — it doesn't just happen. We must work to develop positive ideals that really do make a difference in our ability to do our best. A winning attitude constantly accents our strengths rather than our weaknesses, our desires rather than our fears. 'It's that dynamic spirit in our heart and soul that says, I can, I will, I must, regardless of the odds. I will get the job done within the letter and the spirit of the rules.'"

He wrote for several minutes in his notes.

"Gary — even after understanding this view of doing our best, most of the time we still don't do it. Even though our focus is right and we apply the basic fundamentals of success, we still don't do our best most of the time, and the reason is THE EDGE.

It's that slight edge that makes all the difference in our performance. It's that third side of the coin. Most all of us know it and talk about it, though we really don't understand it and apply it. But when we do, exciting things start to happen that bring out the best in ourselves more often."

"I still haven't gotten it; what is THE EDGE?"

"We are talking about the third side of the coin, the third definition of 'best' — that is, *GIVING IT OUR BEST SHOT.* This is the one area we have the most control over. Most people consider doing your best and giving it your best shot as the same, but they're not. You see, when we don't do our best or as good as we think we should, we get down on ourselves very quickly. We become frustrated, self-critical, and lose confidence. All this leads to the fear of failure, and we end up actually trying too hard, resulting in lower performance levels. When we concentrate on giving it our best shot, we just reload and keep aiming and firing, while adjusting and adapting ourselves to each changing situation. We continually enjoy the challenge of the moment, the excitement of each opportunity; and the by-product is that our best will come out a higher percent of the time. This is where THE EDGE is — *it's in the process.* Let me give you an excellent example of adjusting and still giving it your best shot."

It was Christmas season and the parents of Jason, a young seven-year-old boy, asked him what he wanted for Christmas. He quickly went and got his box of baseball cards and took out one stack of them. He showed them to his parents and said, "I want to be one of these." His dad replied, "But son, you have a baseball suit and a ball and glove already." Jason's eyes lit up and he said, "But dad, look at these cards." He laid out a dozen or so pictures of great baseball hitters. Jason continued, "I want to be a great hitter and for Christmas I would like a model of a major league bat and major league baseball just like these pros play with." His mom and dad looked at each other and smiled as they saw the excitement in their son's desire. The next day the dad went to the sporting goods store and ordered a youth model of a major league bat with Jason's name on it and a major league baseball.

Christmas morning came. Jason was so excited he was up very early. He slipped downstairs in the quietness of the house, and as he looked under the Christmas tree, there it was. His major league bat and ball. He picked up the bat and saw his name printed on it: JASON JOHNSON.

Wow! He quickly put on his little baseball suit, went to the garage, got his bike, and put his glove and new bat and ball in the side baskets. Jason then rode off in the clear, crisp, sunny Christmas morning to the baseball park a few blocks away from his home. He parked his bike, took his bat, ball and glove and slid under the fence of the baseball field. He ran to home plate and laid down his glove, putting the baseball in his back pocket. He was now going to pitch to himself by throwing the ball up in the air with one hand, then grabbing the bat with both hands and taking a swing like all big hitters do. Jason stood in the batter's box. He knew all about this; he'd seen baseball on T.V. and his dad had coached him in the backyard. He first tapped the bat against each shoe, like the big leaguers do, pulled on his cap and banged the bat on the plate, taking a couple of practice swings. Now he was ready. He took the ball from his pocket, went through a little wind-up with his arm, and pitched the ball in the air. As the ball came down, he took a big swing and missed, and yelled, "STRIKE ONE." Then in a firm voice he said out loud, "I'm just getting used to the pitcher; besides I'm pitching anyway and I've got two more swings." Jason readied himself again. He wound up — there's the pitch — he swung and missed again. "STRIKE TWO," he shouted and he picked up the ball from the ground. Determination was now in his voice and he said, "It only takes one swing to hit it, all big hitters know that. This is the big pitch." His eyes looked around the empty stands, though in his mind he visualized a crowd there watching him go after the next big pitch. He pulled on his cap, banged on the plate and readied himself for the pitch. Jason wound up again with a slow, deliberate one-handed wind-up. The pitch on the way — he takes a big swing and missed. "STRIKE THREE," he shouted. Our big hitter had just struck out on three straight pitches. There was a moment of hesitation before Jason picked up the ball. He then tossed it up in the air a few times and excitedly exclaimed, *"Maybe not a hitter, but oh, what a pitcher!"*

"When *we really learn to enjoy the process of giving it our **BEST SHOT** in all that we do — we raise the chances of **DOING OUR BEST** more often. This can directly result in our **BEING THE BEST** some of the time. That's **what** the three sided coin is all about.* Gary — heads or tails?"

He looked at me and quickly responded:

"THE EDGE."

Chapter 4

Striving and Arriving

WE had become so involved in our conversation we hadn't noticed that it was now late afternoon. We decided to jog up to the lake to see the sunset — the exercise was just what we needed, and our timing was perfect.

We arrived at the lake as the sun was setting in the multi-colored sky reflecting pinkish hues on the snow-capped mountains. The fluffy white clouds were forming imaginary figures of all shapes and sizes. It was spectacular. We stayed until twilight.

Returning to the cabin, we fixed a tasty homemade pizza dinner, then brought in more wood from the large pile outside and put several logs on the embers of our fire. Sitting in our comfortable chairs, we watched the dancing flames engulf the new wood as the fire once again was crackling and burning brightly.

"Frosty, I really believe I'm starting to understand the relationship of the pieces of THE BIG TIME puzzle we have put together."

"Remember what I said, Gary: 'All of a sudden the true picture of THE BIG TIME will appear.' We still have other important pieces to fit in, and right now, I have one of them — the 'striving and arriving' piece. This piece in itself gives us another paradox. How can we strive and arrive at the same time? Doesn't striving mean trying hard, continuous effort? Doesn't arriving mean getting there, reaching a destination, coming to a place? They do mean these things, yet they can also be happening at the same time. A great example of this is an outstanding short motion picture film entitled "SOLO", which has won many film awards. This film really shares the striving and arriving idea. It's an action story of a young mountain climber climbing a high mountain by himself. There is no dialog, just music, great action, with spectacular scenes. The entire theme of the film is the excitement and beauty of the challenging climb, both up and down. It captures the true fulfillment of the trip, not just getting to the top of the mountain. In fact, during the sixteen minute film, the climber is on top for less than a minute. The rest of the film is of the journey. The climber shares enjoyment of each accomplishment of his adventure and deals with his adversities in a positive, resilient manner as he radiates the real zest of the climb. We can miss this exciting adventure in our own lives so easily in our quest for getting there — wherever there is. Here's a good analogy of how we can miss the real thing when it's right there in front of us:"

> Three men were on a business trip and stopped overnight at a small motel. After filling out the registration card, the desk manager told them that the price of the room was $30. Each man then paid $10, took the key and went to the room. Later the desk manager realized that these men qualified for a special rate of $25, so he gave the room clerk five $1 bills and told him to deliver them to the room where the men had just checked in. The clerk came to the room and knocked on the door. One of the men answered and the room clerk explained the special rate of $25 and handed the man the $5 refund. The man at the door then tipped the room clerk $2 and gave each man $1 back. Each of the three men then had paid only $9 for the room and the room clerk had the $2 tip.

"Now, Gary — where did the other dollar go?"

We both remained silent for several moments and I then said, "As we think through the missing dollar scenario for a while we come to realize that there really is no missing dollar — it's one of those math mind teasers. This example is just like us missing the real trip as we struggle to strive and finally arrive — It all depends on our point of view. Once again, many of us have been given only one model to choose from, like we had with the model of winning. The standard model most people know is the Road to Success. This model is entirely focused on the destination; THE BIG TIME is a place, and the many people who buy into this put all their time and efforts into getting there. They search and search and search for this Road to Success, yet never seem to find it. And do you know why? Because I believe there really isn't a road to success."

"Frosty, everyone talks about the Road to Success."

"I think this so-called Road to Success is just like that imaginary trip people would take to the end of the rainbow, where the pot of gold is supposed to be. But it just isn't there. Don't get me wrong, I believe there is a road, but a different kind of a road. Let's look at it from another point of view in a model known as 'the Success Road.' It is quite different than the so-called 'Road to Success,' and is based on the trip and the quality of living, not on the destination. It doesn't focus on the regrets of yesterday or the fears of tomorrow but on the moment-by-moment, day-by-day trip that exposes the excitement and joy in the natural highs of many ordinary things in our daily life."

"Frosty, I've got another point of view. First off, I haven't found that dollar from the motel yet, and second, if you're going to be successful at anything, you have to have goals, wouldn't you agree?"

"O.K., let's look at goals. There is no question that goals are important in our lives; however, on the Success Road they take a different form. Goals are derived from our dreams and desires which are the long- and intermediate-range targets that give us direction, meaning and purpose. These dreams and desires are very important to have, and yet they can change or modify themselves many times during our trip. Daily goals assist us in moving towards these targets in the various areas of our lives. They are the specific, daily do-it-nows.

The key idea of the Success Road is that there is personal fulfillment in achievements along the way in whatever we do. It's the day-by-day things that make a difference, up close and personal. It's the short segments of the long trip that really count. Like this adventure with the lion:"

Mark was a successful businessman and the president of a new company. He wanted to develop a logo for his company, so he met with his staff and they discussed the many possibilities. Since their company was involved with both wild and domestic animals, the group decided on an animal for their logo — a lion. They also decided that their president should go to Africa, shoot a lion, and bring it back to be mounted. Mark agreed, and immediately started firing a rifle at a local firing range. He practiced every day for several weeks and became an excellent shot at animal targets 200 and 300 yards away. He was ready — he took a jet plane to Africa, joined a safari, and was ready to shoot a lion for the company logo. He talked to a guide who told him he had to be patient, and that it would probably be two or three weeks before they sighted any lions. Mark, aggressive businessman that he was, didn't want to wait that long and convinced the guide to at least take him to where lions had been seen before. Off they went the next morning through the jungle, away from the camp. After several miles they came to some heavy underbrush. The guide pulled back a large piece of brush, and to his amazement, there was a lion! He wasn't 200 yards away, but only 20 yards away.

Mark was thrilled to have a chance to shoot the lion. He took his rifle, aimed, and fired. He missed. He fired again — and missed. The lion charged them. The guide pulled Mark down under a fallen tree trunk as the lion jumped over them and ran off into the jungle. The guide was scared to death, and he told Mark he hadn't expected to see a lion there and that they both could easily have been killed. They carefully worked their way back to camp. All the way back Mark wondered why he had missed the short-range shots at the lion. He had remembered hitting all those bulls-eyes at animal targets at long-range back home. When they returned to camp, Mark got some cans and bottles and stood them up on some stumps and started to practice his short shots. He found he missed more than half the time. He couldn't believe it; these targets were so close he should have been able to hit them every time. He practiced these short shots all day and finally started hitting them on a regular basis.

The next day Mark was anxious to go back where the lion had been. He was ready. The fearful guide explained that 'no way' were they going back to the same location — the lion wouldn't be in that area anyway. Mark decided to go by himself, so he hiked back to where they had been the day before. He pulled back the large bush and sure enough — no lion. He then took his field glasses and surveyed the entire grassy field. He peered from his left to his right. All of a sudden, on the far side of the field he saw the lion — and do you know what the lion was doing?

Practicing short jumps!

Gary laughed and jotted in his notes.

I summed it up by saying, "It's funny when you really think about a lion practicing short jumps. This story illustrates the importance of little things which many people on the Road to Success never notice or take for granted, while others on the Success Road make something out of them — MAKING THE BIG TIME WHERE THEY ARE."

THE GOAL IS NOT AT THE END OF THE ROAD;

THE GOAL IS THE ROAD.

He leaned back and thought about the choices he had made with himself, his family, and his life.

It had now gotten quite late, and we decided to turn in for the night. As Gary rose from his chair, he looked closely at the large picture hanging over the fireplace. He hadn't noticed it before. It was a picture of a mountain. To his surprise, going up to the top was —

A ROAD.

Chapter 5

Is It Really a Good Day?

WE were up early the next morning and took a hike in another direction from the lake. The crisp morning air felt good as we moved through the tall evergreen trees. The sun was just coming over the big mountain peak and we decided to circle around to the lake on our way back. When we arrived, the lake was like a mirror, calm and serene with an occasional fish jumping. Deer grazed at the edge of the trees on the far side — this was indeed a beautiful spot. We returned to the cabin, fixed breakfast, and moved into a small sun room at the other end of it. It was all glass on one side and gave an open view of the majestic mountain.

"Gary, we've covered considerable ground on the SUCCESS ROAD, and our BIG TIME puzzle is starting to fill itself in. But we still can't see the true picture. There is one thing we need to remember." I pulled out another small plaque from my briefcase:

THE SUCCESS ROAD IS ALWAYS

UNDER CONSTRUCTION

"That's the excitement of this road — there is always something going on: adjusting — adapting — adventuring."

He wrote briefly in his notebook and turned the page.

"Gary, when you go into a store to buy something, and you pay for it, what does the sales clerk usually say besides 'Thank you'?"

"Have a good day."

"That's exactly right. 'Have a good day' has become one of the buzz phrases of our time; but do you know, Gary, you just can't have a good day?"

"What do you mean?"

"I mean this 'Have a good day' is analogous to a thermometer. If we were like a thermometer, we would be affected by all the external changes and circumstances around us each day. We would have no control and circumstances would control us. Our mood swings would go up and down like the temperature, and we could get bent out of shape quite easily. While circumstances might indicate that we can't have a good day, we can learn to *'make' it a good day*, and that's our choice. We are then like a thermostat rather than a thermometer, for we set the dial — this is where the control is. We can control our actions and reactions to external circumstances that go on within and around us. By playing the achievement game and the put-up game we can make the day an adventure regardless of what day it is. Some people look at their week like this: Blue Monday, Hump Wednesday, and Thank God It's Friday. The weekend they live for comes and goes, and they start all over again. What a way to live — enduring five days of the week to try to enjoy two. Not very good odds."

"I saw a bumper sticker that said, 'ISN'T IT FRIDAY YET?'"

"People get caught in that weekend mentality and lose so many opportunities for the adventure and challenges of each day in the many ordinary things in life. I have a banker friend whose positive attitude is so contagious that his entire bank staff has caught it, and the bank has truly become an enjoyable place to work. He has a great game on making it a good day. He told me to use the money-game analogy for each day — Yesterday is a cancelled check, tomorrow is a promissory note — but today is ready cash, so spend it! The Bible gives us the perfect perspective; it is found in Psalms 118:24 — 'This is the day which the Lord has made; let us rejoice and be glad in it.' Today is the only day we really live."

Gary looked quizzically.

"You know, far too often, people take life too seriously. They just don't laugh enough. When we don't feel like laughing, that's really when we need to laugh the most, and believe me, we need to learn to do this. I'm not talking about laughing at jokes, situation comedies on T.V., movies, or at someone else; I'm talking about laughing at ourselves. We get so uptight in many situations in our daily lives because we can't laugh at ourselves. When we learn to laugh at ourselves when things aren't going well, it frees us up. We can think more clearly and not be so afraid to make mistakes, and as a result perform at a higher level. A doctor told me one time that you can't laugh and have an ulcer at the same time."

"Many people should have heard that years ago."

"That's for sure — laughter is the sunshine of our souls. Chad is a young boy who will put a smile in your heart, for he's definitely the type that will make it a good day."

Chad wanted to get a part-time job after school to earn some money for a new bicycle. He found out the local newspaper office wanted to hire a young boy several days a week after school to clean up the print shop. He went to the newspaper office after school and noticed that there was a line of young boys waiting to be interviewed for the job. Chad went to the end of the line and asked the young boy there if he would save his place. The young boy told him he didn't need to, for he was the last kid in line. Chad told him that he had counted the boys in line and he was the 25th place, and that if anyone else came to please save it for him. The other young boy agreed. Chad walked up to the front of the line to the secretary and asked if he could borrow a pencil and piece of paper. He also asked her for the name of the manager. She gave the paper and pencil to him, along with the manager's business card. He then proceeded to write a short note. He folded it, returned the pencil and asked the lady to please give this note to Mr. West, the manager. She asked him where he was in line and Chad told her he was the last boy. The woman quickly told him that there was no use giving him any note, that he would hire one of the first few boys in the line; he always had. Chad urged her to give the note to the manager; so she finally nodded in agreement, and he went back to the end of the line.

When the manager came out of his office, the secretary handed him Chad's note. He read it, tucked it in his pocket and started interviewing the young boys. Five, ten, fifteen, twenty boys went in and came out of the manager's office. The secretary couldn't believe he would interview that many applicants for such a small job as this; he never had before. Finally he got to Chad. He went in the office for his interview and came out with Mr. West, who introduced him to the secretary as the latest new employee of the newspaper. She couldn't believe it. Chad was a fine young boy; but so were the others, and he was the last kid in line. She wondered what his secret was to getting hired.

After Chad had left, she asked Mr. West what prompted him to interview all those young boys and then end up hiring Chad. He picked up the note from his desk and gave it to her to read:

> *Dear Mr. West,*
>
> *I'm the 25th kid in line.*
> *Please don't hire anybody*
> *until you talk to me.*
>
> *Thanks,*
> *Chad*

"In an ordinary situation he wouldn't have gotten the job, but his extraordinary actions set him apart. This shows what happens when you feel good about yourself — you are willing to take some risks and give it your best shot in all that you do."

"What if Chad hadn't gotten the job?"

"He knew the odds were stacked against him being the 25th kid in line; and while he may have been disappointed, I'm sure he would have gone out and kept looking until he found one.

Another excellent illustration of the good-day concept is with baseball hitters. Baseball is a long season, and hitters are up to bat hundreds of times. They establish a batting average which determines how good a hitter they are. Here's how this can correspond to our daily lives. Everyday we are symbolically up to bat many times; we hit some, we miss some, some hits go for singles and doubles, others for triples and even some home runs. Other times we fly out, ground out, and even strike out. But we end up each day with a batting average. Let's take an even closer look. Every Sunday during the baseball season, you will find near the back of the sports section a listing of the batting averages and other statistics of approximately one hundred players in each major league. They are listed in numerical order by their batting averages.

If you're in the top ten percent of the hitters, you are batting .333 or better. That's one hit out of every three times at bat. The top hitters in baseball are put out twice for every base hit they get. Those are the top hitters. Trivia question, Gary. Who was the last .400 hitter in baseball?

"Ted Williams."

"Right. His batting average was .406 in 1941. Let's try another one. Who has had the highest batting average for one season in the major leagues since Ted Williams?"

"George Brett — .390 in 1983."

"That's it. You hit it right on the nose. But now let's take a look at the hitters in the lower third of the batting average list. They hit .250 or less. That's one hit out of four. Let's look at the difference between the top .333 hitters and the lower third .250 hitters in ten times at bat. The .333 hitter would have three hits, the .250 hitter would have two hits. Gary, there is the key point: **The difference between these two hitters is only 1 hit in every 10 times at bat.**"

"That's hard to believe — the difference is so little."

"That's for sure. However, we need to realize that the longer they play, the bigger that gap gets. That's why understanding the one out of ten is so important. We're not talking about six hits, four hits, or even two hits; we're talking about the difference of **one hit; that is all it is**. What does that really mean? It means we really should have more .333 hitters! The key to raising our batting average each day is to play the right games, adjust ourselves, and make it a good day. With concentrated focus we can get that one hit each day; one extra effort, one extra struggle, one extra anything — and up goes our average."

"Frosty, too many of us get upset when we don't do everything, or most everything, right the first time. That's like having to get a hit every time up, and I know that is unrealistic. This batting average example really puts this into perspective."

"That doesn't literally mean that for every one thing we do right, we can do two things not so right and still be a .333 hitter; but it does mean that we can adjust to the ups and downs of our daily lives without getting so uptight with ourselves. I talked to a group of doctors one time, and they started laughing when I gave them the .333 batting average illustration. I never had any group laugh at this example before. One doctor finally spoke up, 'Frosty, if we only save one out of every three patients from dying, we wouldn't be in business.' So, Gary, our batting average example is a figurative one, but it's a great one. We have a big plaque on the wall of our locker room that says it all." I pulled out a small version of it:

.333
Go For It!

"Making it a good day is a choice, and regardless of our situation; whether it is physical, mental, social or spiritual, we can enjoy the challenge of this day. However, we must understand that we will be surrounded by lots of thermometer-type people who can't wait for the day, the week, or whatever, to be over. They openly state their put-downs and negative attitudes about the day and its problems. We can play this put-down game with them if we want to — the choice is ours; but this isn't the game to play if you want to be a .333 hitter. Believe me, the put-down game produces a lot of .250 hitters.

"Larry, one of my former staff coaches, illustrates how to make some unusual adjustments to make it a good day."

Larry strongly desired to be a speaker at banquets, clinics, and large group meetings. He was, however, afraid to even try; for he got so nervous and jittery, he just couldn't communicate — he choked. He was an excellent speaker and communicator in the classroom, and to his players as a football coach; but when he got in unfamiliar settings, he was really out of his comfort zone and choked up.

We talked about this several times, and he would go to banquets and clinics with me to observe; but it didn't seem to help him. The same thing always happened when he had the opportunity to speak at these types of events — he choked up. We decided all he needed to do to break this mental block was to give a simple, short presentation in front of a large group of people. We finally found the perfect situation. Larry would introduce the annual Christmas Choir program at one of the large churches in the area. It was a very easy clear-cut opportunity for him.

The day for the event came. The program was scheduled for seven o'clock that evening. All day long Larry was excited, yet nervous. The butterflies were flying in his stomach; but believe me, they weren't in formation. He wanted me to be with him; so with one of our other coaches, I met Larry at the church a half hour before the program. We gave Larry one of our pre-game talks, so to speak, and reassured him he would do great; all he had to do was relax and follow the script. It was a few minutes before the program was to begin. Larry went to the restroom and returned just as the 100-voice choir was filing in. The church was packed with 1,000 people. It was standing room only.

The lights went down and a spotlight went on where Larry was to be. It was front and center, only a few feet away from the first row of pews. After we had a short prayer together with Larry, he walked out to his place — it was game time.

"Now picture this: Larry was wearing a dark blue suit, white shirt and tie. His suit coat was open and he was holding the printed program in his hands. Would you believe the zipper of his pants was wide open? To make matters worse, part of his white shirt was sticking out through his fly."

"Did anybody notice it?"

"We couldn't see it, but it was very noticeable from the front three rows."

Before he said a word, he looked down and noticed his open zipper. Without a hitch, he dropped his program in front of him, leaned over to pick it up, and zipped up his zipper.

"It was a great move. But one little thing went wrong — he got his tie caught in the zipper, and couldn't get it out."

He walked in a bent position to the side room where we were. It was one of the funniest situations I've ever seen, but it really wasn't funny for Larry. It was hard to keep from laughing. We helped get his tie out of the zipper. He was totally embarrassed — he wouldn't go back out to the spotlight. I told him when a pilot cracks up in an airplane, if he doesn't go right back up, he won't fly again. He looked at me quizzically, hesitated, and then walked back to the spotlight.

"The great thing about this was that the people in the first three rows stood up and gave him a standing ovation."

Gary laughed heartily.

"It took real courage for Larry to go back out there in front of all those people, just like it takes courage for each of us to make positive adjustments in our daily lives.

"Remember, success in life is really a choice — are we a thermometer or a thermostat?"

WE DON'T HAVE A GOOD DAY,

WE MAKE IT A GOOD DAY!

Chapter 6
The Double-Edged Sword

BEHIND the cabin surrounded by tall trees was a small basketball court with one basket. Gary and I went out and shot hoops for about an hour. We really enjoyed ourselves playing the classic shooting games: horse, 21, around the horn, and a little one on one. The old shooting eye was still there for both of us — once in a while. We returned to the cabin, cleaned up, and then settled back in the sunroom.

"Gary, what's your definition of pride?"

"Pride is confidence. It's that desire to do a top job in whatever you do."

"That's right, pride is important for excellence. However, it can be a two-edged sword. Pride is like fire — in its proper setting, like we see it here in the fireplace, it has a radiant, warm feeling and gives a sense of relaxation and rejuvenation. However, when it is out of control, as in a forest fire, or a burning building, it is destructive and causes hardships, pain and suffering. Like everything else in life, there needs to be the right combination, and this combination is hard to find. Selfish pride, the other edge of the sword, is like the fire out of control and it becomes detrimental to success.   This comes when people have an exaggerated view of themselves."

"I know what you are saying — some of my acquaintances are like that."

"The one thing about a person with excessive pride is that it makes everyone around him sick — except the person himself."

"This pride guy should be quarantined."

"He should have a sign hung on his back with a big 'I' on it. By the way the middle letter of the word pride is an 'I'. The key is to keep the 'I' in the middle; yet too many people keep that 'I' out in front, waiving the flag for #1, or pointing the #1 finger like Custer's group.

"Let's talk about the other edge of the sword: sharing pride. This is the side that can bring out the best in all of us. It's a special quality that brings out that inner drive and motivates us to give the extra effort to make things happen.   This creates an atmosphere of confidence that is contagious. Vince Lombardi, legendary coach of the Green Bay Packers, gave his team a sharing pride in high-level performance that turned them into champions. The qualities of belief, courage, determination and dedication were taught and brought out through his coaching staff and players. Their commitment to excellence in themselves and each other put the greatest strength in the world behind them — Heart Power — and their successes were a by-product of this sharing pride."

"I can also identify that with your football team, Frosty. When you gave me the opportunity to sit in the press box at several of your home games, I could really see this. I saw your players on the field helping each other up, encouraging each other and congratulating each other. I also saw how involved the players were on the sidelines, doing the same thing the guys on the field were doing. I even saw your players helping up your opponents."

"That's right, Gary. We respect our opponents because we love the competitive experience they give us. We give it our best shot until the whistle blows, then help everybody up, re-group and get ready for the next play."

"That's not the way I've seen many teams play. Some try to intimidate each other after a play; others are cheap-shot artists."

"There are always some of those around; however, when you set the tone of the game by sincerely respecting your opponent and then demonstrating it when the action ceases at the end of a play by helping each other up, you bring class to the competition and raise it to its highest level."

"What if the other team doesn't do it?"

"It doesn't matter. We believe in enjoying the competitive experience, and if the other team is hung up on the macho man stuff, that's their problem. We know it doesn't help them play better; and remember, we are not comparing ourselves to them but to our own best self. As a matter of fact, those phony psych games actually boomerang on them."

"Our coaching staff and players have put our sharing pride beliefs into an acronym called CUP LIFT. Our CUP runs over because we are continually LIFTing up one another.

C *is for challenge.*	We're only as big as our challenge.
U *is for you.*	You are an important member of our team.
P *is for put-up.*	The power of the put-up game.
L *is for longer.*	The longer we play, the better we get.
I *is for I.*	I will give it my best shot.
F *is for find.*	Somebody is going to find a way.
T *is for total release.*	I will totally let go of myself, thereby releasing my God-given talents to be my best.

"We then apply the **MAGIC**. It's another great acronym that really says what we believe:

> **M** - *Make*
> **A** - *A*
> **G** - *Greater*
> **I** - *Individual*
> **C** - *Commitment*

"*Make A Greater Individual Commitment.* When we do this, we will bring out the best in ourselves and others —- that's sharing pride."

He wrote steadily for a few minutes in his notes.

"Many people talk about these things. But until you really believe them, you can't apply the MAGIC and give it your best shot.

"Various people over the years have said to me that football isn't enough like life. I respond by telling them that life isn't enough like football, because when a person builds his life on the positive values that can be learned through playing football or any other team sport, he can be a winner. The sports arena can teach us a lot about ourselves — courage, confidence, discipline, and perseverance, as well as loyalty, teamwork and sportsmanship. These qualities give us that will to succeed — that ability to do whatever it takes to get the job done, regardless of the odds. These are all key qualities in any successful life. Learning these qualities, like anything else, is directly related to the dynamics of leadership.   Unfortunately, there are people in leadership roles in every profession who don't believe in character — in fact they <u>are</u> characters, and their credo is " You've got to cheat to win or if you can't win, cheat." They believe you are never guilty until you are caught, and in their thinking you won't get caught. People who lead others through the use of unethical practices, for personal gain or any gain, pass on a distorted view of success. This is like building a house on sand — when the first storms come, it collapses and the damage is great.   This type of individual undermines the true values of what America and sports are all about."

"Your analogy of life and football was a good one. However, it seems there are people for whom the verdict of the scoreboard is all that really counts — they've got to win, and they don't seem to care how they do it."

"Gary, no team wins every game, but you can be a winner in every game. Knute Rockne, the all-time great Notre Dame coach, left us a legacy of values that are very important for success in football and in life. He stated that to limit a college education to books, classrooms and laboratories is to give education too narrow a meaning for modern times. Rockne believed that one of the most dangerous trends in American life was that we Americans were getting soft, both inside and out; we were losing that powerful heritage of mind and body that once was our most precious possession. That was back in his day, but the same holds true even more today. Competition in our country in any field, under positive and ethical leadership, can counter this trend through the building of the key qualities we have just talked about. Rockne went on to say that without these qualities, 'the most educated brain of man is not worth much.' He realized these were difficult to measure or evaluate; however, his analogy of the diploma was one of the best. Rockne stated, 'No one should be graded on their contribution to our national intelligence until all the results are in, some five to ten years after graduation *when their record and character are not hung on the wall like a diploma, but inside the man himself.*" That's what *walking your talk* is all about."

I handed him a plaque that said it all —

CHARACTER:

OUR

BEST PIECE

OF EQUIPMENT

Chapter 7

A Touch of Class

IT was noontime and we took time out for lunch, then went back into the living room and built one more fire. It started quite easily — sparks turned into flames jumping from log to log as the fire once again burned a golden yellow. Pulling up our chairs and sitting down, I remarked, "You know, Gary, there are people who will sit in front of a cold fireplace waiting for the warmth and comfort it could bring but are unwilling to put any logs on to start the fire."

"Some people just won't make the effort to start anything."

"You are so right. That's why there are so many .250 hitters out there. It takes that extra effort to make things happen. Even though our .333 hitter is a baseball statistic, it transcends other sports and life as well. Take for example Steve Largent, former all-pro wide receiver of the Seattle Seahawks and future hall-of-famer, whom I consider a .400 hitter and one with real class. When he was interviewed on television following one of his outstanding games, they said he was not only a player with talent and great football savvy, but also a player with class. The announcer then proceeded to ask Steve to give a one-line definition of class. Steve gave him one word: *humility*. Steve is humility, he really walks his talk — talented, confident, yet modest and unpretentious; a person who really is a team player. Class means a lot of things, and humility is one of the key building blocks. Character is another one of these. It is integrity, respect, honor and courage. It's all these things wrapped into one.

"Whenever character is mentioned, I immediately think of John Wooden. Many know and remember him as one of the greatest all-time college basketball coaches in history. He certainly was that! However, I am not referring to what he did, but how he did it. John Wooden exemplifies character. There is a saying that goes, 'Your character is what you stand for and your reputation is what you fall for.' John Wooden stands for what I believe American sports and our American way of life should be all about. The graphic illustration of his Pyramid of Success is hung up in many homes and offices throughout our country. The pyramid is made up of 15 character building blocks. At the top, is his definition of success that I believe really puts it in perspective:

**'Success is peace of mind
which is a direct result of
self-satisfaction in knowing
you did your best
to become the best
that you are capable of becoming.'"**

I got up and walked over to the mantel on the fireplace where I had laid my billfold. I pulled out a small card from it and handed it to him. He read aloud,

**PEOPLE DON'T CARE
HOW MUCH YOU KNOW
UNTIL THEY KNOW
HOW MUCH YOU CARE**

"Gary, I believe an ounce of this type of caring and inspiration is worth a ton of information; for when you care, you do inspire and you will find the necessary information you need. Several years ago a company ran a series of full-page inspirational plaques in *The Wall Street Journal*. The only logo or identification on them was a footnote in small type with the company name and address. The response for reprints of these plaques was overwhelming — would you believe over two million?"

"Two million?"

"Yes, Gary, two million. Those plaques were an oasis of inspiration in the desert of information."

"What does caring really mean to you?"

"It means a concern, a genuine interest in another person."

"That's right, for when you truly care, you are concerned. You are interested in others and you will make the time to be with them. Caring motivates us all.

"People are motivated in basically three ways: fear, incentive and love. Fear and incentive are motivators that can produce quick results but soon lose their effectiveness. They are both extrinsic, and motivate from the outside rather than from within. Fear motivation is the old 'Kick in The Pants' stuff. In other words, if you don't do it, you get kicked in the pants. Here is a motivation plaque that fits this mindset:

> ## The Floggings
> ## Will Continue
> ## Until Morale Improves

It's all the 'have-to' kind of stuff. In this style you endure the trip and do what you have to do; but in the end it leads to mediocrity, for there is no extra effort.

"Incentive motivation is the classic 'carrot on the stick.' You see this a lot today, but certain conditions have to be met for it to be effective. The carrot has to be big enough, it can't be too far away, and the person needs to be hungry for carrots. In this style of motivation, you always have to have a bag of carrots with plenty of big ones. In other words, when you give people something extra, they will produce. For a certain period of time the reward system will work; but it has to be in the right situations. Eventually mediocrity will set in when people are doing the right things for the wrong reasons. They are responding for the rewards, not for the genuine reason of doing the best job they can.

"The third type, and I believe the strongest and most lasting, is the intrinsic motivation of love. Love is a basic need of everyone — **a genuine unselfish love** that puts a priority on relationships and develops a healthy resilient rapport among people. What we're really talking about is caring and sharing of yourself with those around you. There is no fear in this kind of love — it creates an atmosphere that brings out the best in ourselves and others, an attitude of 'want-to' and not 'have-to.' It's not always a 'like-to,' and there are times we struggle within ourselves — but, the by-products of sharing make it all worthwhile. Tough love is an essential part of this within both ourselves and others. It is that ability to give and take when confronting the struggles that occur in any relationship. It isn't always pleasant but it has great long-range results. As relationships grow, confidence and trust rise to new levels, bringing about a feeling of mutual respect. When we start being motivated by love, the genuine concern and caring we share becomes another one of the key qualities of class."

I took out a diagram of the **LOVE CIRCLE** and handed it to Gary.

"Frosty, this is in the shape of a football. I never thought of Love in a rough sport like football."

"The caring and sharing of a team and mutual respect for opponents is what makes football the great game it is. Love binds a family, a team, a business, or any organization together like nothing else can."

"LOVE desires to SHARE and sharing takes many different forms which brings us to new levels of fulfillment.

The true joy of HAVING is in SHARING.

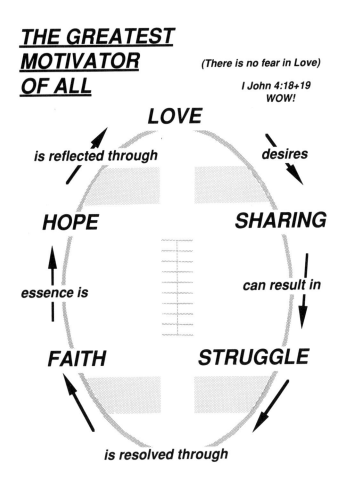

THE GREATEST MOTIVATOR OF ALL

(There is no fear in Love)

I John 4:18+19
WOW!

LOVE

is reflected through

desires

HOPE

SHARING

essence is

can result in

FAITH

STRUGGLE

is resolved through

"SHARING however can result in STRUGGLE due to our own conflicting desires and mood swings. When our eyes are focused on ourselves, we share for the wrong reasons. Many people give up in the STRUGGLE rather than work through it. Tough love is part of this, for there will always be STRUGGLES in our lives — and it's in working through these struggles that we find out who we really are. **The STRUGGLE is resolved through FAITH** — faith in the Lord, faith in ourselves, faith in others. This brings us to new levels of relationships which are built on trust, for there is no tr<u>ust</u> without <u>us</u>. The essence of FAITH is HOPE. **HOPE is what keeps that desire alive within all of us — and this is reflected through unselfish LOVE.**

...FAITH, HOPE and LOVE,
and the greatest of these is LOVE.
1 Corinthians 13:13

"Gary, let me tell you about love and football."

I was a high school football coach for eight years before moving to the college level. During those exciting years we were very fortunate to have some excellent teams and outstanding young men to coach. For three years it was my privilege to coach an

exceptional young quarterback named
Dave Stewart. Dave led our team to several
championship seasons and state
recognition. He was only 5' 9" and weighed
155 pounds, and he didn't have the innate
talent or physical attributes of many other
quarterbacks — but he was a winner and
he made those around him winners. He
worked hard to develop his football skills
and became a fine ball handler, an excellent
short passer, and a motivating team leader.
He was always ahead of the game. His
knowledge was amazing, but above all he
inspired and brought out the best in those
around him. If I could have weighed his
heart, I would have listed him on the
football program at 205 pounds instead of
155, because I know his heart would have
weighed at least 50 pounds.

Dave's family became close friends of
ours during his high school years. He and I
spent many hours together in quarterback
meetings, on-the-field practices, and many
informal talk sessions — it became a special
player-coach relationship. During the
summers of his junior and senior years,
Dave along with several other teammates
and our family attended the Fellowship of
Christian Athletes National Conference in
Estes Park, Colorado. These conferences
were life-changing times for all of us.

Dave continually impressed and inspired me with his humility, his caring, his character and his consistent high-level play — he was class with a capital 'C'.

Dave was not recruited by any colleges after his high school graduation, but he did enroll and walk-on at a state university. As you probably know, walk-ons really don't get many opportunities to prove themselves, so when they do get a chance, they really have to make the most of it. Dave was ranked sixth of six quarterbacks on the freshman team. As the season progressed, several quarterbacks ahead of him got hurt and in the third freshman game he got his first chance to play. He led his team to five touchdowns enroute to their first victory of the season. The next week he again led his team to another big win. At the end of his freshman season, Dave had moved up to be one of the top two freshman quarterbacks. Players just played better with him as their leader. He challenged them, encouraged them and motivated them — his leadership was from the heart and his QB play was outstanding.

Shortly after the football season was over, Dave drove home from college for the weekend. It was a cold, foggy, overcast day and the rain was turning to sleet and ice. A little before four o'clock that afternoon, he pulled into the driveway of his home and went into the kitchen. His mother was on the telephone upstairs and he yelled up to her that he was home; she called down for him to go over to get his grandmother for dinner. Dave grabbed a few cookies and went out the back door, jumped in his car, and drove away. The streets had now become quite slick. His grandmother's house was approximately two miles through town, but less than a mile if you took the back way which he always did. This route went over a marked railroad crossing with no warning signals. As Dave drove down the ice-covered street and was approaching the railroad crossing, a passenger train was rapidly moving toward that same crossing.

There was a shattering crash. The engine of the train hit his car and carried it some two hundred yards down the track before it could stop. Dave was killed instantly.

The word spread fast around the city about the fatal crash, and we heard about it when we returned home several hours later. Donna and I immediately went to the Stewarts' home. I rang the doorbell — and what happened in the next few minutes and the rest of the evening has affected me the rest of my life. Dave's mom opened the door. We looked at each other, hugged for several minutes, and before I could say a word, she said, "Frosty, I knew you and Donna would come — Dave loved you — Dave loved you." Tears started streaming down our cheeks. My heart was pounding and aching, yet filled to overflowing.

Many friends and relatives were coming and going during the next several hours. We stayed until most other people had come and gone and then were able to sit with Dave's parents and share with them. They showed us his scrapbooks and reminisced about the many football games, trips, and meetings we had had together. It was ironic that we had come to share and comfort the Stewarts and they were the ones who were actually sharing and comforting us. It was after midnight when we were ready to leave. We prayed together and Donna and I left with a peace in our hearts that transcended time and place.

The Stewarts' home was directly across the street from the football stadium where Dave had played all of his junior high and high school games. The stadium was a sunken bowl and open at the far end. From their front porch which was high above the stadium, you could see the entire field and actually watch a game. It was like sitting high in the end zone and looking down at the field.

We started down the front walk and looked down into the stadium that was partially lighted by a large flood light on the far end. It brought back vivid memories of the many games Dave and I had planned and played together on this hundred-yard field. The freezing rain had stopped and while it was cold, it was calm. Donna and I went over, unlocked the stadium gate and went and sat high in the seats on the home side — looking at the field — thinking and praying for Dave and his family. It made us realize the awesome power of God's love shown through people. I saw for the first time that in this rough, tough, sometimes violent game of football, there can be a special kind of love. That night I prayed that I could share this love, a love that was given to me by my young quarterback.

I got up and looked out the window for some time. Gary understood my deep emotional involvement in this personal experience. I wiped the tears from my eyes and returned to the chair.

We both sat and looked at the fire for some time. I reached down, slowly pulled two tan parchment copies from my briefcase, and handed one to Gary.

What Is Class?

Class never runs scared. It is sure-footed and confident in the knowledge that you can meet life head-on and handle whatever comes along.

Jacob had it. Esau didn't. Symbolically, we can look to Jacob's wrestling match with the angel. Those who have class have wrestled with their own personal 'angel' and won a victory that marks them thereafter.

Class never makes excuses. It takes its lumps and learns from past mistakes.

Class is considerate of others. It knows that good manners are nothing more than a series of petty sacrifices.

Class bespeaks an aristocracy that has nothing to do with ancestors or money. The most affluent blueblood can be totally without class while the descendant of a Welsh miner may ooze class from every pore.

Class never tries to build itself up by tearing others down.

Class is already up and need not strive to look better by making others look worse.

Class can "walk with kings and keep its virtue, and talk with crowds and keep the common touch." Everyone is comfortable with the person who has class — because he is comfortable with himself.

If you have class, you don't need much of anything else. If you don't have it, no matter what else you have — it doesn't make much difference.

Chapter 8

A Ride in the Country

"**G**ARY, have you ever seen the F-CARD?"

"What's the F-CARD?"

"Here it is"

> **FINISHED FILES ARE THE RE-SULT OF YEARS OF SCIENTIF-IC STUDY COMBINED WITH THE EXPERIENCE OF MANY YEARS.**

"Why do they call it the F-CARD?"

"Well, you are supposed to tell me how many F's are on the card."

He read the card over several times.

"Is this a trick or something?"

"No, I just want you to tell me how many F's are on the card."

He paused. "O.K., three."

"Are you sure?"

He counted them again. "Yes, three."

"That's interesting."

"What do you mean, that's interesting?"

"Eighty percent of the people who see the F-CARD say that — but twenty percent of the people see more than three."

"The 20/80 rule, huh? How many do the 20% see?"

"Six."

Gary counted the F's again.

"They must have looked at a different card — there are only three on this one."

"O.K., Gary — look at the word *of*."

He reread the card. He couldn't believe it. He had read the card and counted the F's a half-dozen times and missed seeing the three F's in the three *of*'s on the card."

"Why didn't I see these?"

"There is a blind spot in our awareness — a gap in our vision field. The reason we don't see them is because we learn to read by phonetics, word sounds. The letter F in *of* sounds like a V; and as a result, we see it, we read it — but we're not aware — *of* — it."

"That's a puzzling one. It's hard to believe I missed seeing them."

"The reason I used the F-CARD was to show you how easily we miss many ordinary things that are right in front of us. When we really learn to take ordinary things in our lives and make something out of them we create many natural highs. We see so much more, do so much more, and enjoy so much more. However, that all depends on your point of view. Let's look at Max's point of view:"

Max started a company in the garbage business and really made a difference through dramatic changes that affected his staff, his customers and the city. He changed the entire image of the job. First, he hired people and trained them in positive attitudes and the team concept, as well as specific techniques of the job. Max changed the vocabulary of his business and started with his people, naming them sanitary engineers. He had them wear sharp blue jumpsuits with their names on them and a bright red baseball cap with the company logo on it. He had a fleet of shiny white trucks trimmed with red and blue that were washed daily. As part of the company service, they supplied brightly colored red, white and blue receptacle containers for their customers. Max gave bonuses to employees for customer relation responses and efficiency ratings. The company distributed a one-page quarterly newsletter keeping their customers informed of the importance of conservation and the environment. There were various other things that he did that were out of the ordinary — however, the key was to make his employees feel good about themselves and in turn treat others with respect. At first the company was laughed at and joked about, but that soon went away, and in its place came respect for a job well done. But the bottom-line was, <u>they just did it</u>. The company received numerous community service awards for excellence. Max's company developed pride in their operation, a sharing pride of performance. On the side of their white trucks, they had this one-liner:

OUR BUSINESS IS REALLY PICKING UP

"Gary, that's taking a so-called ordinary job, and making something out of it. This is a fine example of what one person can do who is really committed. He used the **MAGIC** we spoke of earlier: *Making A Greater Individual Commitment.*

"Here's another one, only this is about a guy named Joe who never went to work a day in his life:"

Joe was an employee of a power and light company for over thirty-five years. He worked at the foreman level on an outside line crew. He had been given opportunities for advancement in the administrative branch, but he always declined these, for he loved what he was doing. He enjoyed the daily challenges of his position, and his crew responded with high-level performance. Joe would share with his crew the big difference between problems and challenges. "A problem," he said, "is a negative way of looking at something. The idea of a problem seems to focus on the ways we can't do it rather than the ways we *can* do it. A challenge, on the other hand, is a positive approach to each situation. A challenge motivates us to find the ways we can do it; and when we think like that — we overcome obstacles and difficult situations that others may have believed impossible."

Joe would always have several new entry-level employees put on his crew, for he always taught them well and gave them a valuable lesson in life. So many times the employees would gripe and complain about their jobs — ordinary, boring things that they had to do. Their attitudes would become negative, and they would just endure each day. After several weeks, Joe would sit down with his new crew and talk with them about how important their attitudes were to their daily lives. He asked them how they got ready for each day. One young man replied, "I get up, do my personal things (shave, shower, etc.), listen to the radio, eat breakfast, glance at the newspaper, grab my lunch, get in the car and drive to work." The other young man agreed that he did about the same thing. Joe then said that your attitude at the beginning of the day is so important. They then asked Joe what he did that was different to make his attitude on the job so positive. Joe looked at them and said, "Guys, I do the same things you do, with one big exception." Joe then went on to explain that he would get up in the morning, do his personal things, listen to the radio, read the paper while eating breakfast, then take his lunch, go outside, get in his car, and **TAKE A RIDE IN THE COUNTRY**. Both young men responded, "When do you go to work?" Joe answered, "I don't go to work, I always go for a ride in the country." The men looked at each other. "You see gentlemen, **THE RIDE IN THE COUNTRY** is my work; and by approaching each day that way, I have learned to enjoy the challenges and make each day a good day, regardless of the situation."

Gary saw how both Max and Joe *were really doing it; they were —*

MAKING THE BIG TIME

WHERE THEY ARE !

Chapter 9
Contented Cows

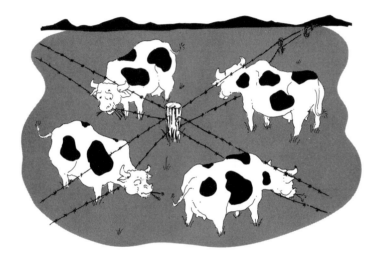

"**W**HAT would be the caption for this cartoon?"

"THE GRASS IS ALWAYS GREENER ON THE OTHER SIDE."

"That's right—those cows sure aren't content."

"Frosty, who wants to be content? If you are content you will fall behind in the success race."

"Gary, most people don't really know what race they are in — especially the most important race of all: THE HUMAN RACE."

"I didn't think of that as a race."

"Most people don't either, for the term in this case does have a different meaning. However, in many ways it is the same race. Our journey through life is a progressive trip (race), and we need to get our focus right as a member of the human race before we enjoy the competition in the success race. This 'grass is greener on the other side' mentality creates much anxiety in our society. It prevents people from making the most out of their present situation. Understanding the real meaning of being content is crucial to the whole idea of MAKING THE BIG TIME WHERE YOU ARE. I agree that contentment, as most people know it, is not a popular term today. It takes on the meaning similar to what you said — of being satisfied and complacent, laid back, with no real desires, goals or ambitions and not even competing in the success race."

Gary nodded.

"Let's look at contentment from a different point of view — from another group of cows. The Carnation Milk Company has used a classic one-liner about their product for years:

The best milk comes from contented cows —
Our cows are content.

"The Carnation Company knows and understands the importance of contentment. Now catch this: The Carnation Cows are content. By being content, they are able to perform at a high level, giving us some of the best milk there is.

You don't do your best and then become

content;

You *are* content, and then do your best.

"There is a big difference."

We got up, stretched and went to the kitchen for cookies and a cup of coffee. Sitting at the kitchen table, I picked up where we had left off.

"Gary, being content comes from the inside of a person; it's from our own heart and spirit. When we are content within ourselves, we can get up each morning and look forward to the challenge of the day, and then get on the success road. The big question is, How do we become content? Let me see if you can tell me."

I had just finished making a presentation at the Coach of the Year clinic when a group of coaches came up to talk more about it.

There was one young coach who shared with me about his coaching and how he had tried to do many of the things I had talked about, but felt he really wasn't making any difference in the lives of the young men he coached. He finished by saying, "But Frosty, I'm just a coach from a small school." I asked him if he wouldn't mind waiting for a few moments until I finished up, then I would like to sit down with him and talk more about coaching. He agreed, and after I finished visiting with the other coaches, the young coach and I went out to the lobby and sat down. I told him I had coached at a small high school in the Midwest, and as I looked back, those were some of the most fulfilling years of my life. I told him that the most important coaches in a young man's life are his junior high and high school coaches — for this is where the seeds are planted in a young boy's mind and body. Most of the time we don't see the fruits of these seeds; but believe me, they will bloom in ways we don't even realize.

I went on to tell him about Archie Griffin:

Archie was the great All-American running back at Ohio State and the only two-time winner of the coveted Heisman Trophy, which signifies the top college football player in the nation. When he received this prestigious award, they asked him who were some of the most influential people in his life. He mentioned his family, a few others — and his high school coach. You see, Archie was from a small high school like the one you coach at. He was a small boy during his junior high and early high school years, but he was fast and shifty. He became discouraged and was going to quit football to concentrate on track. His coach sat down with him and in what had to be one of the most important talks of his life, affirmed him and encouraged Archie to continue to turn out for football. He then gave him a plaque that Archie has kept all through his high school, college and professional career. That talk with his high school coach really did make a difference in his life. The plaque his coach gave him read:

IT'S NOT THE SIZE OF THE DOG IN THE FIGHT; IT'S THE SIZE OF THE FIGHT IN THE DOG

"After spending time with this young high school coach, encouraging him and sharing with him about Archie Griffin, his excitement for coaching and teaching became evident again. He realized that in his situation, he really could make a difference—he could be content and MAKE THE BIG TIME WHERE HE WAS."

"Frosty, you made this young coach feel good about himself and where he was, and really made him aware of the great opportunity he had to influence young kids."

"That's right — hopefully, I gave him back some pride, a sharing pride both to himself as a person and the position he held as a high school football coach. I encouraged him to be the coach that he really can be. The put-up game that we have talked so much about is an integral part of building contentment. You see, we can't give away what we don't have, so the put-up game has to start first with ourselves — and that is not easy, for the way we talk to ourselves can be very negative."

We took our coffee, a handful of cookies and moved back into the living room to our fireplace spot.

"We are all a combination of positives and negatives, and the way we think and talk to ourselves as well as others reveals the kind of person we really are. We need to be aware that we have been conditioned by many negative forces in our society, and that our past experiences have a strong influence on us. An interesting example of this is that most people talk about things they didn't do rather than the things they did. "

I took a cassette tape from my briefcase, then reached over and put it on top of Gary's head. He looked at me quizzically. "These past experiences are symbolically stored in our mind like a collection of video and audio tapes like the one sitting on your head. We have looked and listened to them in our head over and over again for years. The ironic thing about this is that we didn't choose many of these tapes. In fact, you didn't choose the tape I put on the top of your head right now. Many times these tapes were dictated by time, place and other people who chose them for us. For example, we didn't choose the time in history we grew up in, where we lived, or which social status we were born with. We didn't choose our physical characteristics, our name, or our genetic talent potential. We also didn't choose many of the attitudes we have — we actually let others do it for us. Some were good, but many weren't. It would be interesting to go back in our mind's eye and edit the experiences of our past, but, this is very difficult to do.   The real pay value is to use our power of choice and select what we record on our tapes from now on."

He tilted his head forward, and the cassette tape fell into his hands.

"That's a very unique way to explain this."

"Rather than being our own judge and jury that convicts us when we make mistakes, goof up, or just don't do it, we now start playing the put-up game with ourselves. We need to look at what is right or almost right in ourselves and reinforce it. This doesn't mean we ignore areas in our life that we need to improve; on the contrary, many of these areas will improve as a by-product. When we start to focus on the positive and act on it, many negative things begin to disappear. Let me give you a good example. We had a running back who fumbled the ball quite often. We constantly reminded him, 'Don't fumble'; which is actually the put-down game. We finally realized this and changed to the put-up game—and told him to 'hold onto the ball.' You know, he had only one fumble the rest of the year. We should lock on to what we want to do, not on what we don't."

"You know, Frosty, all these concepts we've been talking about are really pretty simple."

"Yes, they are simple to understand — *but believe me they're not easy to do. Remember it's a state of the heart.* The heart is willing but the flesh is weak. So many times we gain new insights into our behavior. We desire to change, but oftentimes we don't. We revert back to our old habits, just the way we've always done it. It's like washing our feet and putting on dirty socks. Remember when we talked about the way you see yourself being directly related to your ability to put someone up?"

He flipped back in his notes, "Yes, that's when we talked about the Birthday Game."

"Birthday game?"

"You know, blowing out or lighting each other's candles, the put-down or put-up games."

"That's a great way to put it. When we can let go of ourselves and start playing the Birthday Game by lighting candles each day, with no return expectations — it just happens — we all shine brighter. It's like a self-fulfilling prophecy that relates to how we see ourselves and others. Most importantly, it's a biblical one from Proverbs 23:7 — *'For as a man thinks within his heart, so he is.'*

"I've got a sad yet intriguing story about a young man who went to work in the railroad yards of a large midwestern city:"

It was a big railyard with multiple tracks and hundreds of railroad cars being moved in and out each day. The young man's job was to fill out a standard checklist on the condition, type, code number, etc. of each car in his section of the yard and file it with the yard foreman at the end of the day. Each man in the crew worked alone and independently. Mid-morning of the second day on the job he came to six refrigerator cars that had come in the night before. He noticed one of them was leaking, so he lifted the arm lock and slid open the door. He jumped into the car, took his flashlight and shined it at the leaky end. At that moment a switch engine sent several other boxcars rolling down the track and bumped into the end of the refrigerator car with a strong jolt that caused the door to slam shut, and the arm lock to fall in place. The young man was locked in the empty refrigerator car. He knew in his mind that survival for very long in this type of car would be impossible, because of the low temperature and lack of oxygen. Working alone he also knew that no one would know he was in the car, and believed his chances of his being rescued were slim and none. He took his pencil, and over a period of time wrote three comments on his clipboard.

The next morning the yard foreman noticed that the young man was not at work. He checked and found the man had not filed his reports the night before. He took several other men from the work crew and started to search the young man's section of the railyard. Each section was quite large and had over one hundred cars in it.

It was late morning when they came upon the refrigerator cars. They opened them one by one, and when they opened the door of the last car; there was the young man — he was dead. The yard foreman picked up the clipboard and read the three comments that were written there.

* *I'm locked in this refrigerator car and I can only live for about 24 hours.*

*   *I can only live for one more hour.*

*   *This is the last line I will ever write.*

"The irony of this story is that the freezing units in the refrigerator car were shut off, and the temperature in the car never got below 40 degrees. There was sufficient air in the car that a person could breathe for at least three days. This young man did not freeze or suffocate to death, he died because he didn't keep his hope alive. He just gave up. This is the key—to keep hope alive in ourselves and others, and that is a choice. Whether we think we can or think we can't, we're usually right. You know, many of our past habits of thought are so strong that we find it hard to let go of them. We're much like a particular breed of monkey in Africa. These monkeys love sugar and are captured in a very unique way. Metal jars with the opening just the size of the monkey's hand are securely buried in the ground with the top sticking out. A sugar cookie is placed in the bottom of each jar. Within a day, several monkeys are trapped with their hand in the jars clutching the sugar cookie. They pull and jerk, and pull and jerk; but can't get their hand out."

"You've got to be kidding?"

"No, they can't get their hand out as long as they hold onto the cookie, for their clutched hand is bigger than the opening of the jar."

"But all they have to do is let go of the cookie."

"That's right."

"Then why don't they? Are they too greedy?"

"They could be, but that's not the real reason. Would you believe they just didn't know? In many ways we are just like these monkeys. We don't let go of many of our past habits that have us trapped. Until we become aware of these, we don't know what is causing us to get caught, and therefore can't MAKE THE BIG TIME WHERE WE ARE."

"Frosty, this in a way is like getting our hand caught in mom's cookie jar when we were kids."

"There is one big difference: We really did know, and our Mom helped us let go of the cookie in a very firm, but friendly way. She let us know what we already knew: Stay out of the cookie jar!"

Gary smiled, looked down and noticed he too was holding a cookie. He thought to himself, "Isn't that ironic; just like the monkeys. I've been holding onto this cookie without knowing it." He opened his notebook and started thumbing through his notes until he came to the two-page summary he had made of the BIG TIME puzzle:

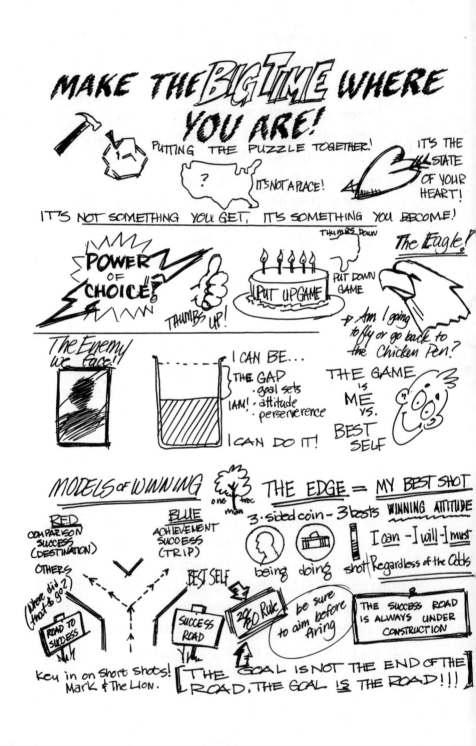

He closed his notebook and thought to himself. Frosty had shared an entire new thought process with him: a different way of thinking and looking at himself and the world around him. He had heard some of these things before at meetings and seminars, but then it didn't seem to have any real value. In the tough, competitive success race, he didn't see how you could think, feel and act like this and still be a winner. He now knew more than ever — you really could. Looking again at his closed notebook he realized the wealth of material he had to build on. It could be his new playbook for not only the business game but also his family, and his own game of life.

We hadn't spoken in some time. Gary was in deep thought, and I was mesmerized by the enchanting fire. He broke the silence by saying, "Frosty, you really do believe all this, don't you?"

"I sure do. I don't know any other way to live. I've MADE THE BIG TIME WHERE I'VE BEEN for as long as I can remember. I believe these concepts that make up this BIG TIME puzzle are worth far more in my life than any fleeting fame or fortune, and I try to live by them each and every day."

"Do you remember the race we talked about earlier?"

"You mean the HUMAN RACE?"

"That's right. When we are content with ourselves, we can be in the HUMAN RACE, the Success Race, any race, and enjoy the trip by MAKING THE BIG TIME WHERE WE ARE.

THERE IS NO ONE ELSE

IN THE WHOLE HUMAN RACE

WITH YOUR KIND OF STYLE

AND YOUR KIND OF GRACE."

Chapter 10
It's Your Call

I T was now late afternoon, and we were getting ready to secure the cabin and start for home. It had truly been an exciting two days for the both of us. I told Gary there was one more thing I wanted to show him. We went to the kitchen and sat down at the table.

"Do you remember what I said about the BIG TIME puzzle when we first came?"

"You said that when we put all the pieces together, suddenly the true picture of the BIG TIME would appear."

"Well, here's the complete puzzle." I opened a small box on the table and started taking out the pieces, one by one. This was a different kind of puzzle. It was a paper puzzle and you stuck the pieces together with scotch tape. I laid out all the 50 pieces and a roll of tape. He could see right away that some of the pieces were the features of someone's head and face.

"Am I supposed to know the person in the puzzle?"

"You will figure that one out as you put it together."

Gary quickly began taping the main pieces of the puzzle together. He worked for some time and as the total face started to appear, he recognized it.

"Frosty, it's a picture of me! It's from one of our business brochures."

"That's right. I had taken the picture of you from your brochure, enlarged it on the copy machine and cut it up to make this puzzle."

Gary finished taping all the pieces of the puzzle together.

"So you're telling me, I'm the BIG TIME?"

"You called it. Just like the three-sided coin in the coin flip, only now you're in control. When you get it all together — you have THE EDGE—you do MAKE THE BIG TIME WHERE YOU ARE."

"That's very clever." Gary looked again at the completed puzzle of himself and noticed in the lower right hand corner a poem, framed in a mirror type design. He read it aloud.

THE MAN IN THE GLASS

When you've got what you want
in your struggle for self
and the world makes you KING for a day,
just go to the mirror and look at yourself,
and see what THAT man has to say.

It isn't your parents or friends or your wife
whose judgment upon you must pass:
The fellow whose verdict counts most
in your life,
is the one staring back from the glass.

Some people may think
you're a straight-shootin' chum
and call you a wonderful guy.
But the man in the glass says
you're only a bum
if you can't look him straight in the eye.

He's the fellow to please, never mind all the rest,
for he's with you clear to the end.
And you've passed your most dangerous
and difficult test
if the man in the glass is your friend.

You may fool the whole world
down the pathway of years
and get pats on the back as you pass.
But your final reward will be
heartache and tears
if you've cheated the man in the glass.

"Frosty, you don't know what these two days have done for me. I've learned so much more about you and your BIG TIME idea, more about appreciating God and nature—even how to watch for falling rocks. I've also learned a powerful set of success principles and much more about myself and my place in life."

"Gary, if I've helped you just a little in seeing the great adventure that life can be everyday, then it's all been worthwhile. The real pay value of MAKING THE BIG TIME WHERE YOU ARE is that it brings more joy and fulfillment into your life — you do perform at a higher level in whatever you do, and you do feel good about yourself as a person. You see, I gain through your gain. It's God's math: The more you divide, the more you multiply.

"One more thing: Pick up the puzzle and turn it over."

He picked up the scotch-taped puzzle and turned it over.

"Why it's a map of our country, all fifty states."

"That's right, Gary, and *when you put the man together — the country takes care of itself.*"

He smiled — the point had become clear, very clear. He thought to himself: "When we learn how to feel good about ourselves, we then take ordinary things in our lives and make something out of them, creating natural highs. East—west—north

— south — city — country— large — or small…
you do
MAKE THE BIG TIME WHERE YOU ARE —
IT'S NOT A PLACE,
IT'S NOT THE STATE OF YOUR MIND —
IT IS THE STATE OF YOUR HEART."
We cleaned up the cabin and I went outside
leaving the front door open while Gary went to the
fireplace to pick up his notebook. He stopped and
looked again at the picture of the mountain road
over the fireplace. He did a double-take and
thought, "Am I seeing right? What is this?" He
looked intently at the picture for several minutes.
The single road to the top of the mountain that he
had seen before now had divided into two roads
half-way up, one road angling left and the other to
the right. He couldn't believe his eyes. He knew
these two roads were not in the picture before.
Then he thought, "Could this be another one of
those blind spots, like on the F-CARD?" It couldn't
be. He was sure there was only one road there
before. But he was also sure there were only three
F's on the card too. How could this picture have
changed? How did he now see for the first time
two roads, when before he was sure there was only
one? His thoughts flashed back to the eagle. Once
the eagle knew it was an eagle, it chose to fly. He
realized it was now his choice. He knew there was
a whole new world out there on this Success Road,

exciting and yet in many ways strange, risky and unknown — time seemed to stand still.

As he turned away from the picture to go, he noticed a small silver cross on the floor beside the big chair where Frosty had been sitting. He picked it up and walked outside, locking the front door. Frosty was sitting on a large tree stump looking up at the mountain. As Gary got close he said, "Is this yours?"

"Yes, it is," I said. "I carry it in my pocket all the time. It must have fallen out. Thanks for finding it." I gazed at the small cross in my hand for several moments, knowing WHO is the centerpiece of my BIG TIME puzzle. Looking up, I said, "You know Gary — these concepts that make up the BIG TIME puzzle will work for anyone — at any place, in any race — if they know the puzzle's true picture, understand how the pieces fit together and really apply them. However, I believe there is an deeper spiritual meaning to the BIG TIME relative to my own life. Hopefully that meaning is reflected by my light shining before my fellow man, and that whatever good works they may see will bring praise to my Father in heaven." We again looked at each other for several moments.

As we pulled onto the mountain highway starting for home, it had become twilight. A deep pink hue still lingered in the western sky. I could sense that Gary was absorbed in his thoughts, as we hadn't said a word for some time. Coming around the curve into the canyon, we could see that the giant fallen rock had been broken into smaller pieces and much of it had been hauled away. The highway was now clear. Our breakaway which had started so dramatically with the big rock was now ending with a pile of smaller rocks. And to my amazement, laying on top of them was

a hammer and chisel.

Continuing on the downgrade of the mountain pass, the lights of the city appeared, twinkling and shining like stars. We would be home in approximately forty-five minutes. Breaking the silence in the car, I said, "I've got one more story I'd like to share with you."

My voice brought Gary's thoughts of the past two days back to the present. After several seconds, he responded, "Frosty, I want you to know that our breakaway trip has truly been a mountaintop experience. It has made me realize the awesome power of choice. It has caused me to reflect on the many choices in my life I have made, and to think about the challenging ones I will make."

"That's just what this story is all about:"

There were two junior high boys who always walked home together after school. They would take the same route home through the city park which was several blocks from their school. There was an old man who sat on one of the green benches along the park sidewalk. Every school day the boys would go past him. As time passed the boys developed an acquaintance with him and found him to be very friendly and intelligent. If fact, he answered every question they asked him. The boys looked forward to talking with the old man each day and to playing the question-answer game. They would ask their teachers for some hard questions in all the various subjects: math, science, history, literature. Day after day, they would ask the old man two questions, and he always had the right answers.

One day on their way home the boys realized they didn't really have any hard questions for the old man. However, on their way through the park, one boy spotted a small baby bird that had apparently fallen from the nest. They looked around but couldn't see where it had fallen from. All of a sudden they got an idea for two questions that they knew the old man could not correctly answer. The one boy was to have the small bird in his hand behind his back. The two questions would be: "What do I have in my hand?" and "Is it dead or is it alive?" There was a possibility that the old man could answer the first question correctly, but there was no way he could the second; for if he answered that the bird was alive, the boy would crush the bird and show him it was dead. If he answered that the bird was dead, he would open his hand and show him that it was alive. They finally had a question the old man could not answer correctly.

While the boys were anxiously talking over their plan, the old man noticed the boy pick up the small bird. As the boys approached, they were extremely excited and were ready to ask the old man their two questions. After greeting him, the boys were ready. The first boy asked the old man what his friend had in his hand, behind his back. The old man paused and then answered, "Your young friend has a small bird in his hand." "You're right, as always," said the first boy. The boys then looked at each other with glee and nodded their heads. The second boy with the bird in his hand asked, "Is the bird dead or is it alive?" The old man thought for a few moments, leaned forward on the park bench looking into the young boy's eyes, and calmly said —

"THE ANSWER IS IN YOUR HANDS."

The Put-Up Game

Affirming — Appreciating — Complimenting —
Encouraging — Praising

Brad Westering — whose love and inspiration challenged me to put these beliefs and success principles into book form. Without his energy, special talents, and contributions this book would never have become a reality.

Brad, I love you.
You are Class with a capital C.

Deniece Westering, Scott and Susan Westering, Stacey and Gary Spani, Holly and Jim Johnson, Sue and Greg O'Neal —for their love, belief, and encouraging support as they live their lives Making the Big Time Where They Are. They also read and reread the numerous drafts of this book and shared their insightful comments and bottom-line feedback.

Family, you win the three-sided coin.
I love you — thanks for the great memories.

Layne Nordgren—my friend and creative computer wizard who put all this together and made it Big Time.

Layne, awesome job.

Shannon Krutz — for her typing and computer talents and tireless efforts in assisting me in putting together the first drafts of Big Time.
Shannon, great second effort.

Thomas Womack — top gun editor of Questar Publishing whose special talents made this book Big Time.
Thomas, you are a real Pro.

Terry Marks — a former collegiate football player of mine whose belief in this book and outstanding talents in graphic arts made our bookcover say it all.
Terry, a Big Five to you.

To the hundreds of players and the coaching staffs whom I've been associated with over the years —
A Big Five to you for your inspiration and perspiration in making THE BIG TIME where we were and where we are.

Acknowledgements

page:

9 The "Power of Choice" idea is adapted from "How to Use your greatest power to change your life" by J. Martin Kohe, in: , *University of Success* by Og Mandino (New York: Bantam Books, 1982) pp. 114-117.

24 "Custer's Last Group Photo" is a "Far Side" cartoon by Gary Larson, and is used by permission.

32 "The Enemy We Face" is by Frosty.

33 The "Potential/Performance Gap" idea is adapted from *Your Attitude is Showing* by Elwood N. Chapman (Chicago: Science Research Associates, Inc. 1983) pp. 42-43.

52 The film *Solo* is a production of Pyramid Films, Santa Monica, California.

80-81 The Knute Rockne statements are from the film *Knute Rockne, All American* a production of MGM/United Artists.

84-85   The John Wooden quotes and "Pyramid of Success" are from his book *They Call Me Coach* (Waco, Texas: Word Books, 1985) pp. 88-89, 198.

88-89   The "Love Circle" illustration is Frosty's.

96   "What is Class?" is from *The Edge,* a collection of quotes, poems, and selections edited by Howard E. Ferguson (Cleveland, Ohio: Great Lakes Lithograph Company) p. 1-1.

127   "The Man in the Glass" is also adapted from *The Edge,* p. 1-15.